SILVER BIRCH
Book of
QUESTIONS & ANSWERS
a useful pocket reference for enquirers and
psychic study groups

edited by
Stan A. Ballard and Roger Green

SPIRITUAL TRUTH PRESS
London, England

First published 1998
Reprinted 2001

ISBN 0 85384 100 4

Printed in England by Booksprint

FOREWORD

In his own obituary, which he wrote before his passing at the age of 79 on July 17th 1981, he revealed that he was told by Estelle Roberts' Red Cloud – a spirit guide for whom he had the greatest admiration – that in a previous incarnation he had made a promise to reincarnate and devote his life to spreading Spiritualism. Though he had no knowledge of that life or promise, events certainly conspired to make that possible.

Maurice Barbanell was born to Jewish parents in a poor area of London's East End. His mother was devoutly religious but his father, a barber, was an atheist and so their son heard many arguments about religion during his early years. His father always won, and his son adopted the same outlook, which later changed to agnosticism.

Yet, after hearing about Spiritualism from a speaker at a social and literary club of which he was secretary, Barbanell refused to start the debate by putting an opposing view – one of his other duties – because, he explained, he had made no personal investigation and therefore his opinions were valueless.

This impressed the speaker, who invited Barbanell to attend a seance in which a medium, Mrs Blaustein, was entranced by various spirits of different nationalities. He was not impressed. Indeed, on his second visit, he fell asleep. Apologising, and believing that either boredom or tiredness had been responsible, the other circle members informed him that he had not been asleep but had been in trance and a Red Indian had spoken through him.

With the encouragement of famous Fleet Street journalist Hannen Swaffer, Barbanell founded *Psychic News* partly as a vehicle for the guide's teachings. But, because he knew he would be criticised for publishing his own mediumship in his own newspaper, Barbanell did not reveal to his readers for many years who was channelling the wisdom.

Silver Birch spoke regularly at Barbanell's home circle and the proceedings were always recorded in shorthand. There were a number of differences in style and procedure between Barbanell's own journalistic efforts and the way in which Silver Birch communicated, as Barbanell himself observed:

FOREWORD

THERE are a number of possible reasons why you are reading this book. The first and most likely is that you are already a "follower" of Silver Birch and have found his great wisdom and spiritual insights of benefit in your life. In which case, you will welcome this new compilation with open arms.

Maybe you have been given this book by a friend who believes its message of love, in this world and the next, will inspire or comfort you. If so, you will not be disappointed.

Perhaps you chanced upon it on a bookshelf or saw it advertised, then curiosity got the better of you. Well, after reading its pages, you may also decide that "chance" played no part in the decision and that some form of spiritual guidance has brought you and this book together.

Whatever the reason, I propose to say nothing about the book's contents – since Silver Birch's words speak so powerfully for themselves – except to congratulate the authors on their labour of love. What a splendid idea to take the published teachings which have appeared in several books and collate them in a way that makes Silver Birch's words so accessible and meaningful.

Instead, I would like to tell you briefly about Silver Birch – the spirit guide whose words are faithfully recorded here – and Maurice Barbanell, the London medium who channelled that wisdom. After all, without such an explanation, many new readers will be puzzled about the teachings and their source.

Barbanell was the founder and editor of a weekly Spiritualist newspaper, *Psychic News*, and for half a century devoted his life to spreading spiritual knowledge through its columns and those of other publications with which he was associated.

DEDICATION

THIS dedication by Silver Birch is taken from "More Wisdom of Silver Birch", edited by Sylvia Barbanell and published by Psychic Press Ltd.

The seed of truth cannot grow where the heart is hard and the mind is stony, but can flourish only where there is a receptive soul, one who is ready to receive truth and to follow truth wherever she leads.

Before you can be so inclined, before you are ready for truth to dwell in your midst, you must have endured some of those experiences which life provides in order to make you ready for truth.

When you had those experiences you may have thought that life was bitter and harsh and unkind, that you were forgotten or lonely, or neglected, and fate had dealt you a very hard blow. But the soul grows through adversity and the pure gold emerges after the processes of crushing and refining have taken place.

If you are about to read the words that follow, then you can say, with all sincerity, you are ready for truth. That does not mean you are called upon to accept all that is written here if the words strike disagreement in your mind. Reject everything that is contrary to reason; discard everything that is foreign to your common sense.

I am only a human being just as you are, but I have trod a few more steps along the roadway of life and I have retraced those steps to tell you what lies ahead of you when you cross the threshold of death to enter the new and wider life that is your inevitable destiny.

So approach truth with humility and with reverence, for with these qualities she will be a welcome guest in your life. Encourage her to stay, for she brings with her assurance, certainty, understanding and, above all, the priceless gift of knowledge which endures for all time.

INTRODUCTION

T HIS book has been compiled because we feel that there is a need for those who are enquiring into the spiritual and psychic side of life, to have at hand a reference containing answers to all the many questions they are very likely to be asking in their search.

We would have wished to have had some such handy reference ourselves when, years ago, we started a psychic study group. What better reference could be made – free from all the misconceptions which can arise or the differing interpretations which can be found within the framework of Spiritualism – than the philosophy and teachings of that great guide known as Silver Birch?

The questions and answers, and statements and responses, which appear in this book have been extracted from some twelve Silver Birch books which had been published by early 1986 (see list opposite). Repetition has been inevitable since the same questions were asked time and again over many years and in grouping them under subjects we have tried to keep to the original wording with a minimum of editing. We have, therefore, occasionally included similar questions because Silver Birch's answer to one is more expansive than another and put together they give a wider view.

Producing this book has been a means of rededication for us and if our efforts can be of help to one enquirer to find the light, then all will have been worthwhile.

Stan A. Ballard
Roger Green

FOREWORD

"In my working life I use words every day. I have never yet written or dictated an article with which I was satisfied when I read it. Inevitably I find, when looking at the typed material, that I can improve it by altering words, phrases and sentences. No such problem arises with the guide's teachings. These flow perfectly, requiring usually only commas, semi-colons or full stops. Another interesting aspect is the occasional use of words that I regard as archaic and do not form part of my normal vocabulary."

But who was Silver Birch? A psychic artist depicts him as a serious-looking Native American Indian with a single feather and compassionate eyes. But there is evidence to suggest that this was simply a convenient *persona* behind which a far more spiritually-elevated soul hid in order that those who read his words would judge them not by the name that was attached to them but by the wisdom that pervades every sentence.

Those of us who knew them both were well aware of the differences in the way they spoke and the words they used. They both had spiritual missions and they fulfilled them admirably, particularly when working together in their unique two-world partnership.

This, as you are about to discover, has provided us with simple, uplifting, comforting and inspirational answers to the questions we all ask, from time to time, about life and its purpose. And they are needed now more than ever before as we prepare for the challenges that will confront us in the 21st century.

ROY STEMMAN
Chairman
Spiritual Truth Foundation
December 1997

CONTENTS

God – The Great Spirit

Q *How would you describe God?*

IT is impossible to give you a complete picture. God is infinite. All language, concepts and pictures must be finite. The lesser cannot include the greater. You can obtain some idea of what the Great Spirit is like by looking at the universe. See how it is regulated by natural law, where provision has been made for every facet of life, even though these manifestations are multitudinous in their variety. Whether it be minutely small or majestically mighty all that lives, moves and breathes, all that exists, are controlled by natural law.

Nothing is outside the orbit of natural law. The seasons follow one another, the earth rotates on its axis, the tide ebbs and flows. Whatever seeds you plant, what will grow is contained within it; it will be true to its nature. Law reigns supreme. Every new discovery, whatever it may be, wherever it may be, is controlled by the same natural law. Nothing is forgotten, nothing is overlooked, nothing is neglected. What is this power responsible for it? It is infinite. It is not a magnified man, the Jehovah of the Old Testament. It is not a deity who is full of vengeance and sends plagues because of displeasure. It is not a capricious, wrathful deity. History and evolution show that the world slowly moves forward, upward, revealing that the power behind it is beneficent. So gradually you get this picture of infinite love and wisdom that rule all, that govern all, that direct all and are within all. And that I call the Great Spirit.

Q *Would you say there is as much of God in all of us as there is anywhere?*

THE Great Spirit has no existence apart from the totality of the Great Spirit which is manifested in all creation.

3

[To Silver Birch, the Law is God and God is the Law]:

There is no personal God apart from the one human beings have created; there is no personal Devil apart from the one that human beings have created. There is no golden heaven, no fiery hell. These are the imaginings of those whose views are limited. The Great Spirit is the law. Know that, and you have learned life's greatest secret, for once you realise the world is governed by unchangeable, unbreakable, immutable, omnipotent law, you know that justice is done and none can be forgotten in the great scheme of creation.

Jesus – (The Nazarene)

THE Nazarene is one of the hierarchy behind all the directives we receive when we leave your world occasionally to fortify ourselves to cope with our missions and to glean more of what it is we have to achieve.

I have a great reverence for Jesus, the Nazarene, a wondrous example of what the power of the spirit could achieve when divinity assumes human form and gives to those available simple but profound teaching that love is a power that solves all problems when people allow themselves to be animated by it.

The Nazarene demonstrated the same spiritual phenomena that we make available today, because their operation is due to the same natural laws which always have been, which still are in existence and will continue to be so.

Having attracted the multitudes by what were wrongly called miracles, he taught the great truths of the spirit – love thy neighbour as thyself; do good to those who hurt you – the essence of all religions.

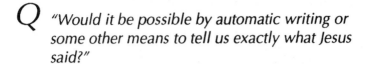

Q *"Would it be possible by automatic writing or some other means to tell us exactly what Jesus said?"*

I don't know. The difficulty is that no one recorded the utterances of the Nazarene at the time and so memory would have to play its part. His main teaching was the gospel of love. "Love thy neighbour as thyself", "Do good to those who hurt you". Love is the fulfilling of the law. What else is required to help mankind? Love is the highest expression of the spirit. Love is what the Great Spirit has to offer. Love is what we offer you.

The object of the Nazarene's mission was to demonstrate spiritual reality. If the Nazarene were to appear in your world today and to repeat what he said 2,000 years ago, I doubt if anyone would listen.

The value of prayer

Q *Is it important to pray?*

THAT depends on the prayer. The aimless repetition of words merely creates ripples in the atmosphere, but those who pray with their hearts and with their souls, seeking in prayer closer unity with the Great Spirit, seeking to make themselves useful instruments for his manifestations, emerge, because of prayer, stronger and more fitted to be His servants. The act of prayer, the revealing of oneself, the opening of the heart, binds us all together in unity.

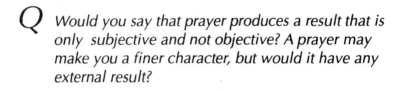

Q *Would you say that prayer produces a result that is only subjective and not objective? A prayer may make you a finer character, but would it have any external result?*

TRUE prayer should enable you to equip yourself for service. Prayer is the means by which you attune yourself to higher forces. I do not mean by prayer repeating the words that others have written without a realisation of what they mean, but praying with the soul and the mind, with an earnest desire to reach out to the highest the soul can attain. Then, filled with the inspiration that comes as a result of the prayer, you emerge stronger.

Q *Is it of any use praying for somebody else?*

YES, true prayer is never wasted, for thought has potency.

Q *Have the prayers of a healer engaged in absent healing any real effect?*

YES. I was answering your question as it referred to individual prayer, but it also has universal application. By prayer you are releasing psychic energy, and this can be used by guides.

Q *Is it possible through prayer to enlist the help of those in the spirit world when otherwise that help might not be available?*

IF you pray with sincerity, you make yourselves, because of the act of prayer, accessible to higher forces. The mere act of prayer opens up the soul. You must pray with your hearts, souls and minds. Mere requests are not prayers. Prayer, truly understood, is a great spiritual exercise. I can best explain it all by saying that prayer should always be regarded as a means to an end, not the end itself. There is only one prayer – that prayer is, "Teach me how to serve" – there is no greater work, no greater love, no greater religion, no greater philosophy than that you say, "I want to serve the Great White Spirit and His children". It matters not which way you serve, whether by bringing the truth of the spiritual part of the Law, or whether you feed those who are hungry or take away all the darkness in men's hearts. It does not matter which way, as long as you serve.

The more you learn how to forget yourself and to serve others, the more you help to develop the spirit – that is, the Great White Spirit – within each one of you. It is all very simple, but they build churches and say many strange things. They use long words which I do not understand, and have ceremonies which they say help religion. But all I know is that you must go and lift up those who are falling, give sleep to those who are weary, food to those who are hungry, drink to the thirsty, new light to those who are in darkness. Then the laws of the Great White Spirit are working through you.

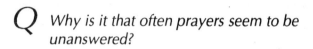

Q Why is it that often prayers seem to be unanswered?

IN everyone there is always a war going on between that part which is human and that part which is divine. When that part which is divine wins, then you feel at one with the Great Spirit. When the human part triumphs, then you feel disheartened.

Often you have to be guided not into the paths for which you think you are fitted, but into those paths where you can be used to give the greatest service. Every day and every night there comes to this house a band of spirits. Every one of them has given up his right to progress in order to build here conditions so that one day it will be a circle of light, with its illumination radiating into all the dark places of the earth. Beside that mission, the little troubles of earth are nothing.

Whilst there are people who have no place to put their heads, who have no homes, and have to sleep under the skies of the Great Spirit, with His stars as their only light, their bodies exposed to the storm and the rain, and others who do not get sufficient food to sustain them, do you think the troubles of any one of you are important in the sight of the Great Spirit?

I only ask you to remember that you are all helping the Plan of the Great Spirit, that great and wondrous design in which each one of you is helping to weave you own little pattern. One day the whole fabric will be revealed and every race and every colour will have its part. Then it will become a perfect universe.

What takes place in the silence, when nothing seems to happen, is but a part of the embroidery being woven. Day after day, and night after night, the work goes on, everyone helping to weave a mighty fabric which will one day cover all the children of the earth.

Sometimes you ask for things which are not good for your soul, which will only retard your progress. Those things cannot be given to you. Sometimes you ask for things which your soul has not earned. They cannot be given to you. Sometimes you ask for things which are already in preparation, ready to be poured into your midst when the right time comes. You must understand that the Great Spirit knows already of the unspoken prayers of your heart.

 Does prayer, as recited daily in churches, avail anything?

IT depends on the one who prays. If it is a prayer of the lips, then it is but an empty waste of sound. If it is a prayer from the soul, a prayer of earnestness and aspiration, a prayer that desires to reach out to the Great Spirit, then the very desire gives it wings which carry it into the heights of the realms of spirit.

Q Would the prayer of a little child, for example, be of any use in curing a drunken parent?

ALL sincere prayer carries with it a power. How far that power can be transmuted into a material result depends on many conditions. It depends, in the case that you give, upon the soul of the man, whether that power can touch his soul, or whether he is so far removed from spiritual things that no spiritual thing can touch his soul. I cannot say yes or no to that question.

Q *But it would have some effect?*

ALL prayer which is prayer, which is aspiration, which is desire for service, for knowledge, for light, for wisdom, for guidance, all that prayer is part of the soul's evolution. Your mind is part, not of the body of matter, but of the spirit, the Great Spirit, and it has powers which belong to the Great Spirit. But before you can use those powers you have to learn through your soul evolution. Otherwise, they cannot be revealed to you.

Q *Are prayers heard by an individual in spirit, or must we postulate a power which can respond only to vibrations which harmonise with itself?*

PRAYER is the expression of the soul. Let me make that clear. It is the yearning of the soul which cries out for light, for guidance. That very act, of itself, brings an answer, because it is setting into motion the power of thought. It is the cause which attracts a reply, which is the effect. There is no need for any spirit to wait for you to pray, because the quality of your prayer immediately attracts all those on the spiritual plane which your prayer can reach, according to the evolution of your soul. And naturally their power – because they decide to serve your world – adds to the power which you set up. You have set into motion waves of thought which are part of the spirit. This enables the force of the universe to work in accordance with your evolution. That means that you have made yourself accessible to those forces which can reach you.

According to the evolution of the people who pray, it may be necessary for them to fix their minds on some ideal. If that helps the soul, I would not deny it. But the Great Spirit, the laws of life, the natural laws of the universe, these are the things that matter. Because the Great Spirit is perfection, the laws of the Great Spirit are perfect. That part of the Great Spirit that is within you is perfection, seeking to express itself. As you allow it to express itself, through prayer, through service, you are allowing the Great Spirit which is within you to express itself. All things, prayer, service, whatever you seek to do that uplifts a soul, help in your evolution.

Q If everything is governed by inexorable law, what is the use of praying to the Great Spirit, for is not prayer a request that the Great Spirit should interfere with the law of His own ordaining on behalf of the one who prays?

THAT is not a prayer as I understand it. Prayer is the desire of the soul to reach out to the Great Spirit. Prayer is the desire to express the Great Spirit and that act enables the soul to express itself and to reach out to planes which before it could not reach. There is no injustice. There is no favouritism. It is merely that the soul equips itself so that it can express more of the Great Spirit and thus receive more of the bounty of the Great Spirit. The bounty of the Great Spirit is infinite and your soul is infinite as you learn to express its infinity.

Q Why do we ask God to forgive us our sins: for if the Law is broken does not the penalty follow?

FORGIVENESS does not enable you to make the adjustment, for you must pay the price. But when you pray for forgiveness you are beginning to put yourselves into harmony with the laws of the Great Spirit, for you are beginning to look within yourself and to examine yourself, and that is when real progress begins.

Q Is it to the natural law that we should pray?

NO, you pray to the Great Spirit which is within and without. You strive through attunement and aspiration to establish a closer unity with that power. Your prayer should always be a desire for more illumination, knowledge, wisdom and understanding. And that prayer will always be answered because the very fact of its petition is helping you to express the inner divinity.

Q *Sometimes we know that other people in your world are helping in certain things. We do not pray to them. How do they become aware of our request?*

SINCERE prayer finds its target. When you really pray, and I mean pray and not ask for something to be given to you, your prayer finds its target. The unfailing magnetic law of attraction works. You build with your prayer a bridge over which that answer can come.

Q *Can we speak direct to the Great Spirit? If so, is the Great Spirit within ourselves?*

YOU are the Great Spirit. The Great Spirit is you. The difference is not in kind or in essence but in degree. The Great Spirit is the acme of perfection, for which you will infinitely strive. So the Great Spirit is within and without. When you express qualities of divinity, love, tolerance, mercy, compassion, charity, you are communicating with the Great Spirit because the Great Spirit is being communicated through you.

Q *What about those who don't pray, and are in the depths of despair? Because they don't believe there is a God, is there no help for them?*

IT doesn't matter if you believe the Great Spirit has no existence. This will not trouble the Great Spirit.

Q *But would they get help? Here is someone incapable of prayer or believing, for various reasons, in God. Yet he is in terrible trouble and needing help.*

THE ability to receive help does not depend on a belief or disbelief in the Great Spirit. It depends on the stage of mental and spiritual evolution reached. This determines what you will receive because you are fitted to receive it. This is cause and effect, which is the natural law.

Q *Do you wait until people have invoked God's help before trying to help them? Or do you simply leave them or help them irrespective of whether they have asked for help or not?*

IT is impossible because of the efficacy of natural law for anyone or any form of being to be forgotten in the divine scheme. The natural laws are so perfect that they embrace all. Nothing and nobody is outside them. You cannot be overlooked by the Great Spirit. Your needs are always known. If you pray, you will get the help that is available according to the mental and spiritual stage you have reached at that moment.

Q *Do days of prayer have any effect in the spirit world?*

ONLY in so far as people are of one mind for one little while. True prayer comes involuntary from the heart. It is not an organised automatic means of addressing the Great Spirit.

Q *Would there be any point in Spiritualists holding a day of prayer?*

THERE is no virtue in those calling themselves Spiritualists unless they are living in their lives the implications of the truth they have received. It is not what a man designates himself that matters, it is what he does.

Q *Is there any answer to prayer?*

SOMETIMES, but it depends on the prayer and motive. Often people pray for things which in the nature of the request cannot be given to them, for they would interfere with their own progress or disorganise their own outlook on life. Prayer is not asking for something and then here we hold a council and say yea or nay. Prayer is attuning yourself to the higher realms so that you yourself provide the conditions so that the response can sometimes come.

Q What is the function of prayer?

IF we draw a distinction between selfish requests and true prayer, then we will get an understanding of how the true prayer operates. Obviously selfish requests cannot be called prayers because they have no real value. No-one in realms beyond your earth is interested in purely selfish requests that want more possessions, more money or more houses. These will not add one iota to your spiritual nature or increase your mental development. But there is the true prayer which springs from the soul; the prayer which in itself is a spiritual exercise; the prayer which desires to obtain a closer fusion with the power that is behind all life. In this kind of prayer you have what is the equivalent to a spiritual introspection, aware of your shortcomings and imperfections you are automatically releasing some of the latent energy within yourself and enabling your prayer to have its answer, because you are creating the potency by which the prayer can be fulfilled.

Sometimes I have said that the best answer to many prayers is to disregard them completely, for if the requests were conceded the individuals would be far worse off. But real prayer, that emanates from the soul, that desires greater knowledge, greater understanding, greater strength, the prayer automatically attracts its response. It creates a vibration, and along that vibration can travel the help that is required for the soul who has reached a stage of evolution when he or she is ready for the next step on the path. When a prayer is made in danger you would automatically attract a blanketing power that can protect you and bring those who are your guardians, not only those who are tied to you by links of blood but others who are attracted by love. They can shield you, as many have found, because they have been helped in times of danger.

Q How does the spirit world regard prayer?

PRAYER is not intended to be a refuse of the coward who seeks to escape his obligations. Prayer is not a substitute for the work that you have to do. Prayer is not a means by which you can escape your responsibilities. Prayer is not a means of outwitting the laws of the Great Spirit. No prayer can do that, neither can it by one iota make any alteration in the unbreakable sequence of cause and effect. You can disregard all prayers which do not spring from a heart which is willing to serve and which is conscious of its obligations and its duties. Having disregarded all those, there are the prayers which, because they are a psychic or spiritual exercise, set into motion certain vibrations which bring responses. Those responses are not necessarily the ones which the man who makes the prayer expects, but they are the natural result of the vibrations he has created.

Q You recently said that true prayer should enable a person to harmonise his will with the will of the Great Spirit, but you did not say how we are to reach this height?

THOSE who find that they cannot pray should not attempt to pray. Prayer is an exercise of the mind and the spirit, a means by which you should harmonise your will with the will of the Great Spirit. If you cannot achieve that in prayer, and you have tried and tried again and again, then it means you have failed. True prayer is the precursor to action. It is the means by which the individual can so harmonise himself with the might and majesty and power of the greater life, that it fills and floods his being and he knows that he is at one with the whole cosmic consciousness and he is strengthened and fortified and ready to give service. That is what I understand by prayer.

Q What is the use of official days of prayer?

PRAYER is not official or unofficial. It is not fixed by days or nights. True prayer cannot be commanded by any source that is outside the individual. There is no value in mechanical prayer, in prayers said by rota. Those who meet from time to time because they have been commanded to do so, or because it is their habit, and read, or have read to them, words that sometimes are so familiar that they make no imprint on their minds – these do not place themselves any nearer the Great Spirit. The Great Spirit is aware of all your needs. There is no need to petition him in large numbers.

The Divine Plan

Q *Can you explain something of the plan that is behind spirit communications?*

OUR work is to give that which has a purpose, a significance, so that, while it demonstrates the existence of law, it also enables comfort to be given and knowledge to be spread. Our work is not only to reveal the existence of laws beyond the physical, but to reveal truths of the spirit ......

Q *Do you consider the maintenance of the British Commonwealth to be advantageous to the world?*

YES, because all that which binds people in unity is to be prized. The world must learn to draw closer together, seeking to find those factors of unity on which it can stand together. That is why we are opposed to those who strive for separation. When the soul is liberated it desires to draw together in harmony all the others in the world.

Q *Why is it that we hear so much about a spirit plan, and yet see such little apparent result of it?*

YOU do not see the results of a plan because you look at these things with the eyes of matter. You judge progress in relation to your own short span of life, but we see progress because we look at things from another plane. We see the spread of knowledge, a greater understanding of spiritual things, a rise of tolerance, an increase of goodwill, a breaking down of barriers of ignorance and superstition and fear and spiritual slavery. It is not as if there were to be a sudden revolution. That could never happen, because all spiritual growth must be slow and progressive. Do not think that there is need for despair. There is on one hand – when you see the growing masses of materialistic forces – but on the other hand there is growing hope as the light of spiritual truth penetrates the fog of materialistic selfishness. And, as long as knowledge spreads, truth will be victorious. We strive to serve you, because we love you. We are not evil spirits, seeking to lure you on to paths of destruction. We do not seek to make you debase yourselves, to practise cruelty or sin. Rather do we strive to make you realise the divinity that is yours, the powers of the Great Spirit that you possess, how you can practise the law of service and help the plan of the Great Spirit.

The Law

[Silver Birch stresses that most of our troubles are brought about by the exercise of our own free will]:

IF you are faced with a war, there will be many who will say: "Why doesn't the Great Spirit stop it? "Why doesn't the Great Spirit prevent it?" Yet, all the time, the people of your world are to blame if they choose to ignore His laws. Do not think that your world can escape the consequences of its actions. We cannot alter the law. What has been sown must be reaped. You have sown selfishness; you must reap the results. Pride, jealousy, envy, greed, malice, distrust, suspicion – all these things, when they fructify, produce war, distress and discord ......

 Is free will limited in the sense that there are definite tendencies of events in relation to individuals?

THERE are tendencies, vibrations, but these are not insuperable. You are surrounded by radiation and influencies, much of which can affect your destiny, but the Great Spirit has provided you with part of Himself, a part of His spirit which, when your free will is properly used according to your evolution, can enable you to conquer all that stands in the way of the fullest expression of that part of the Great Spirit that is within you. For you are the Great Spirit and the Great Spirit is you.

The seed of the Great Spirit is planted within every human soul and, like the seed which is planted in the earth, if you give it that which makes it grow aright, then the little seed will first shoot up through the earth and gradually it will bloom until it bursts into the full beauty of the flower. The Great Spirit has planted the seed within you, but you are the gardener and it depends on your efforts whether and when the fullness of the flower is able to express itself. There is always your free will. If you keep the seed in the darkness and do not give it the light of soul-growth, of charity, of service, then the Great Spirit is not being expressed through you.

Q *What is the value of suffering?*

EVERY experience is part of the pattern of your life. You try to judge eternity by temporal happenings. You see in matter apparent confusion, but you do not realise that a divine thread runs throughout all your lives ...

Do you think that the latent powers of the soul, infinite in their possibilities of expression, could realise themselves without difficulty and pain, without shadow, without sorrow, and without suffering and misery? Of course not ...

[A sitter, whilst on holiday, had taken part in a fox shoot and asked Silver Birch whether it was wrong.]

ALL life belongs to the Great White Spirit, and no one must take it, in whatever form it is.

Q *But the fox had eaten twenty chickens.*

SUPPOSE I gave the fox a gun and told him to shoot you because you had eaten twenty chickens! The Great White Spirit has provided for all his children everywhere. It is man who makes them starve, not the fox. When you can create the fox, or the chicken, then you can take its life away. If it is true that you can kill the fox and the chicken, then it is right for a man to kill his brother. Life does not belong to man. It belongs to the Great White Spirit. Whenever anyone takes it away, he must answer for it some day.

Cause and effect

THE Law is perfect in its operation. Effect always follows cause with mathematical precision. No individual has the power to alter by one hair's breadth the sequence of cause and effect. That which is reaped must be that which is sown, and the soul of every individual registers indelibly all the results of earthly life. He who has sinned against the law bears on his own soul the results of his earthly action, and there will be no progress until reparation has been made for every sinful deed.

The law of cause and effect is basic, fundamental and unalterable because you can only reap what you have sown. Effect must follow cause with mathematical accuracy; it cannot be otherwise. In turn, the effect becomes the cause by which another effect is set into motion, producing another cause. The process is a constant one. The flower will always be constant to the seed.

Throughout the vast variety of the phenomena of nature, everything small or large, simple or complex, follows the law of cause and effect. None and nothing can interrupt that sequence. If effect did not follow cause, your world, the universe and the vast cosmos would be chaotic. The Great Spirit, God, the Deity, the Supreme Power, would not be the summit of love, wisdom and the perfection of all that exists.

The universe is ruled by divine justice. If at a stroke, by reciting some words said to have some religious and spiritual significance, you could obliterate the results of some wrong you have done, then that would be a criticism that the natural law was not perfect in its operation, but unjust because you could change its pattern.

Nature must follow its ordained path, oblivious to man's desire. It has its tasks to perform, and will continue to do so. When man works in harmony he reaps the results. Nature can be profligate in the abundance it has to offer to those who work in harmony with it.

Whatever good you do, you are the better for it. Whatever selfishness you practice, you are the worse for it. You cannot cheat the natural law. You cannot say on your deathbed that you are sorry for what you have done, and automatically obliterate all the effects of the causes you set in motion.

Natural Law

ALL law is part of one vast law. All works in harmony because all is part of the divine plan. The lesson of it is that men and women throughout the whole world of matter must seek their salvation by working it out in their daily lives, and abandon all the false theology which teaches that it is possible to cast on to others the results and responsibilities of your own actions.

Man is the gardener of his own soul. The Great Spirit has provided him with all that is necessary for it to grow in wisdom, grace and beauty. The implements are there, he has but to use them wisely and well.

The infallible law

THE Great Spirit is infinite, and you are parts of the Great Spirit. If you have perfect faith and live your lives right, then you are able to participate in the bounty of the Great Spirit. If every person in your world had perfect faith, then he would receive. If a person were hungry yet had perfect faith, then he would receive the answer.

That is how the law operates. If you learn to attune yourself to the law, the result must come. If the results do not come, that only proves that you are not in tune with the law. Your history books tell you that there have been those from the lowest of the low, the poorest of the poor, who have tried the law and it has not failed them. You must not point to those who do not try it and ask why it does not work.

I will tell you another law. There is nothing you can have in the world of matter without you pay the price. The price of mediumship is increased sensitiveness. You cannot accumulate wealth without paying the price, because if you do that and forget the duties of your own spirit, then you may be rich in the goods of your world but you will be very poor in my world.

Q *Why do many bad people prosper in health and affairs and good ones suffer?*

ALL attempts to judge the perfection of natural law by earthly happenings are a very poor standard of comparison. The earthly life is a very short aspect of a tremendously large life that will continue when the individual has finished with all the affairs of earth. But, even apart from that, is the correct appraisal of human happenings to be determined by the outward show? Can human beings look into the heart, into the soul and into the mind? Can they know the inner life of every individual, the secret thoughts and cares and worries and pains and aches? All that transpires is part of a vast earthly lesson, for every experience is stamped indelibly on the soul, helping it to grow through happiness and pain, through joy and sorrow, through sunshine and storm, through health and sickness.

Q *If the lesson for life is to learn love and compassion, why does nature set such a bad example by allowing predators?*

NATURE does not set anyone a bad example. Nature is an expression of the Great Spirit. The Great Spirit is perfect. The laws of the Great Spirit are perfect. Nature, left to its own devices, will always achieve the right balance and harmony. If man lived in harmony with nature then your world would be a paradise, a kingdom of heaven. There are predators, but that is part of the way nature ensures the survival of the fittest. Yet that is only one aspect of natural law at work. The essence of nature is co-operation. Nature is symbiotic. If you, for example, are a gardener and you prepare your garden and co-operate with nature, the results are beautiful. Man is the predator in your world, the greatest destructive creature that has been known for many millions of years.

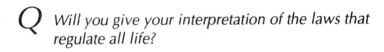

Q Will you give your interpretation of the laws that regulate all life?

WE always render our homage and our tribute to the eternal, natural laws of the Great Spirit, the laws which never fail, the laws which never err, the laws which take care of every being, no matter how exalted or inferior his state may be. None is neglected, none is overlooked, none is forgotten, none is lonely. There are no people who are outside or beyond the scope of these laws. The mere fact of their existence is due to the operation of natural law. Man's laws may fail, man's laws may change, man's laws may be repealed or superseded as growth and development enlarge his vision, as knowledge dispels ignorance, as changing circumstances demands the provision of new ordinances, but there are no additions to the laws of the Great Spirit. There are no revisions. There are no alterations. All the laws that are in operation today have always been in operation and always will be in operation. They are constant and immutable.

Spirit laws

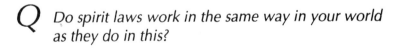

Q Do spirit laws work in the same way in your world as they do in this?

NO, they do not work in the same way because ours is a graded life in which the people who have reached the same stage of evolution occupy the same plane of existence. Thus they do not have the comparison of earth where you have on one plane contrasting experiences. In our world everyone is on the plane to which they have evolved. We cannot have an undeveloped and a highly developed soul in the same sphere of existence. On one surface in your world you meet, day by day, people of differing mental and spiritual attainment. But that is not so in our world, unless we choose to indulge in missionary work and go, comparatively speaking, to lower spheres. Otherwise we meet with our own spiritual equals. When we have evolved, we go on to the next spiritual level. Thus there is not in one sphere the comparisons of existence.

In any case we have no darkness and light, we have no shadows. Those who have reached the attainment where they live in the light of the spirit have the understanding of what the light is, otherwise they could not be there.

Those who have not attained that stage are still in the astral belt where they have the illusion of light and dark. As you unfold greater still, you do not require that comparison. You will have a truer understanding of realities and will know the face of truth for what it is.

When you can get the "wholeness" of a flower revealed to you, because you have the spiritual gaze, that gives an appreciation of floral beauty you could not have in your world because we see the "inside" and the "outside" of everything that exists. There is an infinite variation of colour that you do not have in your world. There are varieties of hues and there is spiritual depth which is the reality of substance that cannot be understood with material perception. We are not subject to the gravitational pull of earth and there is eternal light for us. As your soul unfolds, beauty unfolds for it. Ours is a creative world, self created by those who dwell in it.

Retribution

Q *Is there any retribution on earth for acts we do?*

SOMETIMES yes, sometimes no. The law does not always fulfil itself in your world. It does fulfil itself, because it must fulfil itself. Effect and cause cannot be divorced from one another. The time element depends upon the nature of the cause that will produce the effect. Thus there are actions which will produce their reactions whilst you are in your world, but the spiritual results are mechanical in their aftermath. If one does another harm, that harm is registered on the spirit of the doer. Thus his soul is poor by the degree of harm that he has done. Whether that will be shown in his physical life, I do not know. It depends upon the circumstances, but it is measured on his spiritual life which is the eternal life.

Compensation

THE law of compensation is automatic in its operation. No matter how much your soul has cried out for help and guidance when none seemed possible, you get the richness of the reward in being able to serve others as you were served and the way was shown to you. That is what I tell all healers and mediums.

Compensation and retribution

HOW could divine justice work without compensation and retribution? Is the sinner to have equality of spiritual status with the saint? Of course not. Whatever good you do, you are the better for it. Whatever selfishness you have shown, you are the worse for it. It is you who make or mar your spiritual destiny. It is you who are personally responsible. If on your death-bed you could repent, and by so doing automatically get rid of all imperfections that result from sins committed, that would be a mockery and a travesty.

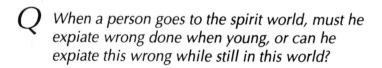

Q When a person goes to the spirit world, must he expiate wrong done when young, or can he expiate this wrong while still in this world?

ALL is governed by circumstance. Whatever wrong you have done you must expiate it. That is an unalterable law, for the soul cannot progress until you have expunged that blot upon it. It does not matter when the wrong was done – in youth, in adult life, in old age – you must put it right, to the best of your ability. When you have done so, or tried to do so, as honestly as you can, you have set in motion another expression of your own soul that cancels the wrong you have done. The law is as simple as that. It is easier if you right, or try to right, an early wrong whilst you are still on earth, manifesting through a physical body. This is the place where the act was committed; this is the place where it is easiest for it to be put right. The longer you delay, the worse it becomes and the effect is to impede your own spiritual growth. Where there is an honest attempt to right a wrong, you call to your aid those who love you, for any effort in the right direction immediately has the backing of those who desire to see you live your life as it should be lived.

Spirit and soul – difference between

THE trouble is semantics, the language of trying to find words that are incapable of explaining the totality of something that is beyond language. Words like soul and spirit are a case in point. You have to define your terms as to what you mean by them.

Let us, for the sake of simple definition, refer to the soul as that portion or particle, that divinity, which comes from the Great Spirit, the infinite spirit.

The spirit is the vehicle of the soul; it will function much more freely once it has separated from the physical body. This is composed of matter; it imposes restrictions on what the spirit can express on earth.

So you are souls with spirits expressing yourself through physical bodies; the personality is that aspect which can be manifested only while you are on earth. It is only an infinitesimal part of the individuality which is the real self; this is because it has no means of fullness of expression while it is cloaked by the physical body.

One soul

Q Are we all part of the same soul?

THAT is very difficult. This is the old trouble when you have to define the words you use. We are all parts of the same spirit because spirit is the substance of life. Soul, for the purpose of strict definition, is individual spirit. So in these terms, all life is one, but spirit being infinite has an infinite variety of manifestations.

Spiritually we are all one, but our souls are individual. In your world people group together. They combine for specific labour or service. In our world there are groupings to achieve functions which are part of the plan. Some of these groupings are not so intact – it is very hard to find words for spiritual conditions – as others. Speaking generally, when there are group souls there is a kinship or affinity between those individual souls in your world.

Spiritual Ambitions versus The Materialistic World

How to balance them?

A similar sort of question was put to the Nazarene. He replied to the effect, "Render unto Caesar the things which are Caesar's and unto God the things that are God's".

Spirit truths

Q *In the New Testament the Nazarene said you cannot put new wine into old bottles. How does that link up with what you have been saying?*

YOU cannot put new wine into old bottles. What you can do is to put old wine into new bottles. You cannot compel the power of the spirit so that it can be fitted into predetermined beliefs. You cannot make spirit truths fit your pattern of belief. You must reject at any time any belief, any doctrine, any form of words, however ancient, that you know are untrue.

Q *Is it possible to give some new truth?*

THERE is no new truth. Truth is truth. Truth is constant and eternal. You can add to wisdom, you can add to knowledge, but you cannot being new truth. Your world has all the truth that it requires for its essential purpose – the fundamental truths of kindness, service and love.

How can the Creator be all loving when He has made nature red in tooth and claw?

FINITE wisdom cannot comprehend infinite wisdom. You cannot answer the problems of universal activity by viewing them only through physical eyes, or by attempting to understand them with your limited mentalities, limited because you can see only a small fragment of a very large picture. It is, of course, true that in one aspect some animals are predatory and that when they require food they have to be "red in tooth and claw". But it is only a very small part of the story because there is a principle of harmony and co-operation at work in the animal world as there is in the human world. It is seen when the opportunity is provided for this law of co-operation to outwork itself. There is also the aspect that man has a responsibility, a great responsibility, towards what is regarded as a lower form of creation, because animals and humans are part of life equally with the tree, the fruit, the flower, the vegetable, the bird. All life moves forward together, or backward together. Thus, if man displays the divine qualities of love, mercy and compassion, then the wolf can lie down with the lamb.

Spirit world – location of

So it doesn't matter where you are, whether you are in a church or in a railway station?

THE world of the spirit has no geographical location. It is round and about you all the time. You are no nearer the Great Spirit in a church, or in a pit, or in an aeroplane.

Q *Is it right to say that there is only one Being or Person that is able to create, and that we have not the power to create anything at all?*

THE Great Spirit is, always was, always will be. All life is the Great Spirit and the Great Spirit is all life. How can you create? But the more you are evolved in your soul, the more you can beautify and improve. The less evolved you are, the lower is your range in the universe.

Nazarene

Q *Have you ever met the Nazarene in the spirit world?*

YES, I have, many times. I have told my friends here about it. Always, when I withdraw from your world, which I do regularly, to attend the gathering where the Nazarene is always present. He is concerned with spreading these truths, of which he was an exemplar on earth, long since buried by those who claim to follow him.

Jesus – His evolution

Q *Was Jesus a human progressed through many incarnations?*

ALL I can say is that the spirit power which expressed itself through the Nazarene is in essence exactly the same as the one expressing itself through everybody in your world today. There are differences in the kind of spirit. All spirit is the same. It is possible for spirit to incarnate throughout the ages in many forms through many individuals.

Are Christ and Cosmic Christ, two aspects of the same existence?

YOU are allowing names to bother you. There is the man Jesus, whose surname was not Christ, and there is what is called the Christ power, the power of the spirit. If you differentiate between the man and the power that animated Him you have the clearest picture of all.

 What is the purpose of creation?

A continual expression is many and varied manifestations of the consciousness which is the Great Spirit.

Creation

Q *What is your view as to the reason for the creation of a universe?*

THERE is a purpose which has infinity in which to accomplish itself. Life always was, life always will be. But life is one long evolutionary climb with peaks to be scaled and other peaks discovered when you have scaled them, and so on, throughout eternity. As you scale each peak, so you rise higher in the scale of your own spiritual values. Man improves, and gradually the divinity within him unfolds and finds fuller and richer expression. The dross of earth is purged away and the pure gold of the spirit begins to emerge. All this is not necessarily a painless process. But this is part of one universal scheme in which contrasts enable you to see the truth.

Without pain you would not appreciate health, without the struggle you would not appreciate the accomplishment, without the shadow you would not appreciate the sunshine. All play their parts in one vast panorama of creation in which all move in rhythm and concert as part of the majestic scheme.

World's creation

Q   *Genesis? Creatures from outer space? There are many theories; we don't really know?*

OF course you are addressing your question to an out-of-space creature! Do not be bothered by what it says in Genesis or in any other book. If it is unacceptable to your reason dismiss it. How did your world begin is what you want to know. Let me say that I have a little more than a theory. I have a little knowledge on this subject. Your world has always existed. It had no beginning nor will it have an end. If you want to quote from the Bible, you have statements like the one attributed to the Nazarene, "Before Abraham was I am".

Spirit has always existed, it was not spontaneously created. It slumbered for millions of years until the rudimental beginnings of life gradually manifested in your world. Life is spirit and spirit is life. It always has had the potentials of infinity.

There were no creatures from outer space to create the beginnings of life in your world. Life was always there, and developed, unfolded and progressed according to the natural laws of evolution that infinite intelligence devised.

Creation of man

Q   *Why is man, who is created in the image of God who is perfect, imperfect?*

THIS is a question of the microcosm and macrocosm. Man possesses in latent form all aspects of perfection. But he has to achieve perfection, which is an infinite process. Man is given the divine perfect spark, but it is for him to order his life so that the spark becomes a radiant flame. The trouble with your world is that man creates God in his image.

Q *Spirit world and physical world. Why is there not just a spirit world?*

THE answer is for me to say to you, "Why do you send children to school?".

This is done so that in their schooldays they learn the lessons that will equip them for the life they must lead when they leave, and are confronted with very different conditions. That is the reason that you come into the physical world. It provides the opportunities and challenges for you to equip yourself for the life you must lead when you leave your world. It is the process of learning so that you are ready for the next stage.

Spirit

Q What is spirit?

SPIRIT is perfect in its origin, spirit possess intrinsically the creative forces of all life. Spirit is not subject to age, infirmity, wastage or to any of the defects that affect the physical body. The line of spirit evolution is from immaturity to maturity. Part of its evolution is accomplished through a physical body, which it has created for that purpose. Spirit is dominant, spirit is the king, spirit is the ruler. But here comes the paradox. There is an interaction between spirit, mind and body, and the body restricts the activity of the spirit on earth because the spirit can express itself on earth only through the body at its disposal.

Q *Who or what is the Great Spirit? Is it love – the spirit or feeling of love in everything?*

THE Great Spirit is the natural law of the universe: the creative force behind all life, whether registered in the plane of matter or in the plane of spirit. The Great Spirit is perfect love and perfect wisdom. The Great Spirit pervades all the universe, whether it is that tiny portion known to you or that larger part which, as yet, has not yet been revealed to earthly gaze.

The Great Spirit fills all life. The Great Spirit is within all beings. The Great Spirit is within all laws. The Great Spirit is the Great Spirit. He is life. He is love. He is everything. How can we, who are but the servants, describe the master? How can we, whose conceptions are puny, describe that which is of immeasurable magnitude?

Q   *In the whole of history has the Great Spirit ever spoken without coming through a spirit entity?*

THE Great Spirit is not a person. The Great Spirit is not a deified individual. The Great Spirit is beyond personality. The Great Spirit is the epitome of law, love, wisdom, truth. The Great Spirit is the law, the infinite intelligence operating ceaselessly in a mighty universe.

Spirit form: what shape do we take in the spirit world?

YOU won't be a ghost, spectre or phantom. You won't be headless. You won't have your head under your arm. You won't have clanking chains. You will be a real individual with a body, and features which enable you to be recognised by others. You will have all the senses which enable you to recognise others. You will have the entire spiritual apparatus which is necessary for you to function in our world.

You will have form, you will have shape, you will have individuality. What you will not have are any of the physical organs, but you will have correspondingly all the spiritual equipment necessary for you to function in our world.

How would you explain the Great Spirit to children?

THAT is not a difficult task if the one who is to do the explaining has a clear conception of the power which is behind all life. For myself, I would point to the divine artistry of nature's handiwork. I would point to the stars, the diamonds in the sky. I would point to the glory of the sun, to the pale reflection of the moon. I would point to the whispering, murmuring breeze, to the nodding pines. I would point to the trickling stream and to the mighty ocean. I would touch every facet of nature showing how each is controlled by purpose, by law. I would add that where man has made any discovery in the field of natural life, he finds it comes within the orbit of law, that its growth is controlled and regulated, that it is part of one vast, intricate, yet harmonious pattern, that order reigns supreme throughout the vast universe, controlling planets and insects, storms and breezes, all life, no matter how variegated its expression may be.

And then I would say, the mind behind all that, the power that sustains it all, the force that controls the vast panorama of the universe and the many other worlds that you have not yet seen, is what we call the Great Spirit.

A spirit view of God

 We are told that God knows when a sparrow falls. How is it possible for God to know of all that happens to all the vast population of the world, not to mention the countless millions who have passed on?

THAT which is called God is the natural Law of the universe. The Great Spirit is within everything. Everything is the Great Spirit. Because the soul knows itself, the Great Spirit knows the soul. Because the sparrow is the Great Spirit, the Great Spirit knows the sparrow. Because the Great

Spirit is the trembling leaf, the trembling leaf is the Great Spirit. Throughout the whole of your world and mine, throughout the universe, even in worlds which are not yet known to you, the laws of the Great Spirit reign supreme. Nothing happens outside those laws; therefore, all is known because all comes within the compass of natural law, which is the Great Spirit.

 You say the Great Spirit is in everything, the source of all things – hate and love, wisdom and folly. It seems to follow that the man who does wrong is acting within the laws of the Great Spirit as much as the man who does right; those who preach the gospel of war and hate as much as those who preach peace and love. No one, in fact, can transgress the laws of God because everything is part of those laws. Can you answer this difficulty?

THERE is perfection and imperfection, but imperfection contains within itself the seeds of perfection, for perfection comes from imperfection. Perfection does not come from perfection, but from imperfection. Life is evolution, it is progress, a striving upward, a development, unfolding, extension, reaching out. What you call good or bad are but stages on the road of life, lines of progress. They are not the end. You judge with an imperfect understanding. You say thus far is good, thus far is bad. That is only your idea. When you are not in relation to those events, you judge them differently. But the Great Spirit is in all things.

Q Then is the Great Spirit responsible for earthquakes?

THE Great Spirit is the law – the law that controls all things. There is nothing in the universe that is outside the law.

I know that earthquakes and storms and lightning puzzle the brains of those in your world, but they are all part of the universe. The universe is evolving, even as those who dwell in it are evolving. The world of matter is far from perfect yet – and it will not reach perfection. It will evolve higher and higher.

Q *Does that mean that the Great Spirit is evolving?*

NO, the Great Spirit is the Law and the law is perfect. But that part of the Great Spirit that is expressed in your world is subject to the evolution of that world so far as its expression is concerned. Remember that your world is evolving, and these things are the signs of its evolution. Your world was born in fire and tempest and is gradually evolving toward perfection.

You cannot say that the Great Spirit is responsible for the beauty of the sunset and the sunrise, for the myriads of glittering stars in the firmament, for all the delightful songs of the birds, and then say that the Great Spirit is not responsible for the storm and the lightning, the thunder and the rain. They are all part of the great law of the Great Spirit.

In that sense, you might argue that the Great Spirit is responsible for those who are depraved, for those who are so unenlightened that they render harm to their brothers in your world. But to each one of you there is given that amount of free will which, as you evolve, you learn to exercise. The higher you evolve in the spiritual scale, the greater can you exercise your free will. You are your own limitation but, because you are part of the Great Spirit, you can conquer all the difficulties and obstacles in your world.

Spirit is superior to matter. Spirit is the king and matter the servant. Spirit reigns supreme. It is the essence out of which all life is made, for the spirit is life and life is spirit.

Q *Is there a Great Spirit apart from His universe?*

NO, the universe is but the reflection of the Great Spirit. The Great Spirit is the system.

Can a fly understand the world? Can the fish realise what the life of the bird is? Can a dog reason like a man? Can the stars understand the sky? Can you understand the Great Spirit, who is greater than all your minds? But you can learn to express your soul, so that, when no words pass your lips and in the silence of your own soul, your spirit reaches out for communion with the Great Spirit. Then you know that He and you are one. It is not possible to express that in language, but it is expressed in the silence of the soul within you and within every soul in the universe.

Q Does spirit need contact with the world of matter in order to gain conscious individuality?

YES. In order to gain consciousness it must incarnate through matter and have the experience of matter. It evolves from matter into spirit. That means that its association with a body of matter enables it to express itself as an individual working through the personality of the physical. Spirit becomes aware of itself after it has incarnated into matter.

Q If so, is the Great Spirit gaining experience through us?

NO. Your evolution cannot affect that which is already perfect.

Q But we are all parts of the Great Spirit. Does not the evolution of a part affect the whole?

IT only affects that part which is manifesting through you, which in itself is perfect, but is not perfect in its expression through each one of you. In itself spirit is perfect. It is the primary substance of the universe. It is the breath of life. In its expression through you it is imperfect because you are imperfect. As you evolve, more of the perfection can express itself through you. You are not evolving the spirit, but you are evolving the bodies through which the spirit can express itself.

Q *Are the bodies through which the spirit expresses itself made of matter in varying form?*

YES. The law is perfect. The law as it is expressed though is not perfect because you are imperfect, and so the perfect law cannot operate through you. But as you become more and more perfect, so more of the law can operate through you. Imagine you have a mirror and a light. The mirror reflects the light, but if the mirror is very poor it cannot reflect all the light. As you make the mirror more perfect, it can reflect all the light. Everything is constantly working itself out in fuller expression. Have I not told you that life is like gold that has to be extracted painfully from the ore, which has to be crushed and purified? Who is to say that the ore is bad but the gold is good?

Q *But surely we all have ideas of what is good and what is evil?*

THESE are but expressions of the moment. They express the stage which has been reached in evolution. When the soul has evolved higher, it will leave them behind. They are but the imperfections caused by a perfect law seeking to express itself through instruments which have deviated from the path. That is why I embrace them all.

Q *Does that mean that God, in the beginning, was not good?*

I know nothing of beginnings. I know nothing of endings. I only know the Great Spirit always has been and always will be. His laws are perfect in their operation. Do you not see that you may have perfect light but, if you strive to reflect it through badly polished mirrors, it does not emerge as perfect? But you cannot say that the light is imperfect, that it is evil. That which your world calls evil is only imperfection, imperfectly expressing the Great Spirit through it.

Evolution

Q *Why are children born with defects, such as being crippled or blind, through no fault or their own?*

YOU must not judge the soul from without. You must not confuse the evolution of the soul with the evolution of the body which it uses on your plane. Although there is what you call a defect, which is caused by the natural law of inheritance from the father or the mother, or both, it does not interfere with the soul's evolution.

You will find, usually, that those who start their material lives with a material defect have in their souls a compensating principal. They exhibit in their character more kindness, tolerance and gentleness to others. There is an eternal principal of compensation. There is nothing that escapes the law of cause and effect. Because those who are the physical parents have the responsibility of providing the materials for bodies of the coming race, it is their duty to hand on that which should be as perfect as possible. But, if they neglect their responsibilities, the law cannot be altered.

Q *If a person is insane and is not a responsible being, how does he get on when he passes to the Other Side, since we are all judged by our characters and the manner in which we have stood our tests?*

YOU confuse the things of matter with the things of spirit. When the brain cells are out of order, they cause confusion in your world. The soul knows its own responsibility even if it cannot express itself in your world because the machinery has gone wrong.

The laws of the Great Spirit work according to the evolution of the soul. The soul is not judged from the standards of earth, but from the standards of eternal wisdom. The soul that wrongs your worldly standard may be judged wrongly from your worldly standards, but if a soul is not responsible, then it is not accounted in the spirit life as in your world. It is the same with those who, in moments of madness, as you call it, take others' lives or their own. They cannot be blamed because the machinery has gone wrong. In my world, the true standard is the standard of the soul's motive. Where that is concerned, there is no mistake.

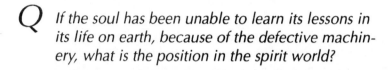

Q *If the soul has been unable to learn its lessons in its life on earth, because of the defective machinery, what is the position in the spirit world?*

TO that extent, it has lost the earthly experience because through the machinery being wrong it does not register its experiences on the soul as it should. It has lost the value of physical experience. But the principle of compensation is at work all the time.

Q *We take into the next world the character we form through passing through the various tests on earth. In the case of an insane person, is he judged by the character he has formed?*

HE is judged only by his own soul evolution and the motives of his soul.

Q *In our world, some children are born in a slum atmosphere of drink, mental, moral and physical filth, and are faced with a life of hard, monotonous labour, while others grow up surrounded by beautiful things and have a delightful preparation for life. How is the unfairness of such cases taken into account?*

THE soul registers its own evolution. People in your world judge always by material standards and not by the expression of the soul. To all, whether born in low or high estate, comes opportunities for service, for the soul to find itself and to express its own divinity. That is the only standard of judgement. All things in your world judged by a material standard, seem to produce inequalities, but the true compensation is the compensation of the soul, which learns to express itself through all difficulties.

Q But why does a bad person have a good time?

YOU judge once again by your worldly standard. How do you know that the soul of the one who has a good time is not miserable, is not tortured, is not racked with anguish and pain? Because you see a smiling face, because you see luxury surround that person? Do purple and fine linen go hand in hand with a satisfied soul?

Eternal standards are the standards of the spirit, if not the world of matter. Otherwise there would be no justice.

Q But surely it is easier for a soul to express good motives when surrounded by a good environment, rather than in surroundings where sin, hunger and everything that is low predominates?

I DO not agree with you, because I see that nearly always the great souls of your world have been born of low estate. All the great masters of your world have come from low estate. The more difficulties that the soul has to struggle against, the greater the soul can become. It is the struggle against circumstances that enables the soul to come into its own. Try to judge not from without but from within.

Q Has the human spirit evolved simultaneously with the evolution of physical life?

IT has evolved, but not on the same pathway, because it was necessary for a certain amount of evolution to take place in the physical body before the spirit could express itself.

Q *As we can progress after 'death' if we will, is it possible to sink to a lower level by sinful motives after 'death'?*

OH yes. There are many who do not progress for hundreds and sometimes thousands of years who are still filled with the desires of earth even when they have passed to the world of spirit. Their lives are filled with greed and desire, and they seek not to understand the laws of the spirit. The things of the spirit make no impression upon them, for they are still of the earth, earthy, and they sink from lower planes to still lower planes.

Q *Does a soul ever sink so low that it is extinguished altogether?*

NO. It may reach a stage where the spark of the Great Spirit within it is but a small flicker, but the light never goes out, for the link which binds it to the Great Spirit is a link forged in eternity. No soul descends so low that it cannot rise. No soul is so high that it cannot descend to help the lowest.

Q *Does the individual lose his or her individuality after passing through the various spheres, eventually merging with the Great Spirit, and then being redistributed in various forms through material and other substances?*

I KNOW of none which has yet reached a stage so perfect that he can be merged into perfection. The more you perfect yourself, the more you find still to be perfected, for you are allowing more of your consciousness to be revealed. Because your consciousness is part of the Great Spirit it is infinite, always stretching out to reach infinity. We know nothing of ultimate perfection.

Q *Is it not a fact that, as individuals progress, they tend to become merged into group personalities, losing their own identity in that of the group?*

NOT as far as I know. What does happen is that, in order for certain work to be accomplished, those who are of one mind pool their knowledge and their resources, allowing one to act as their spokesman on behalf of the rest. While that happens, they all sink their identity into one, but that is only temporary.

Q *Have you any knowledge of the survival of lower animals, other than pets?*

YES, I have. There were many animals which were friends of ours when we lived on earth and who were, to us, what your dogs and cats are to you. These animals, where they learned to express a personality, survived with us. But that survival is not eternal. It lasts only for a time, and then the animal goes on to merge with the group spirit which perpetuates the species.

You must understand that all the children of the Great Spirit, because they have the power of the Great Spirit, can transmit the power to survive the changes called death to those whose consciousness has not yet been expressed in evolution. You can make it possible for the evolution to express itself before its time because of the love that you show.

Q *Apart from pets, do animals survive individually?*

NO

Q *If animals, not pets, do not survive individually, what relationship exists between the Great Spirit and, say, an uncared-for and perhaps ill-treated animal? How does the life of such an animal reveal the love of justice of the Great Spirit, viewing it as a matter between the Creator and the created?*

IT is very hard to explain to people in your world things which are so far beyond their understanding. I have tried to explain that animals, when they pass on, go to join the group spirit, but even then there is a principle of compensation. They are able to work out in divine justice all that compensation which is due to them, but it is on different lines from that of the human evolution. You may as well try to explain what is the difference between a flower that is cared for and a flower that fades and is allowed to fade because it is given no attention. You cannot understand the law behind that, but there is one just the same.

Q *Are animals compensated individually?*

NO, in the group. The suffering brings forward the evolution of the group.

Q *If there are in one group animals that have been ill-treated and animals that have not, and the group is treated as a group, it is difficult to understand how part of the group can get more compensation than another part.*

EACH group is made up of those who have gone through similar experiences.

Q *Do you mean there are separate groups for those who have been badly treated and those who have not?*

THERE are divisions that make up a whole, as you have a body with many forms of cell life as part of that body.

Q *What reason is conceivable for the existence of the lowest forms of life, and how is their creation and necessary destruction compatible with a universe ruled by love?*

MAN has free will. He can make the world of matter a Garden of Eden, if he chooses, by exercising the power which the Great Spirit has given him and by using the wisdom which the Great Spirit has given him to discern between the things that are right and the things that are wrong. If, instead of making it a Garden of Eden, he chooses to allow dirt and filth to exist, why should the Great Spirit be blamed for the results of man's filthiness?

Q *Where is the evidence of God's goodness and love when creation has come through a blood-red track of carnage in its evolution?*

WHY do they look only to one little corner of the picture and not at the whole picture? Because there is evolution, is that not proof of the God of love? Has that never occurred to them? Because you evolve from the lower to the higher, is that not proof that the force which is behind the Law is a force of love?

Q *Why does God allow earthquakes and volcanoes?*

WHEN you say: "Why does God allow?" you must remember that you are trying to question the operation of natural law. I only seek to teach the law and the experiences I have had of the law. What you call earthquakes are part of the cleansing process in the evolution of the material world. The world of matter has not yet reached a stage of perfection in evolution.

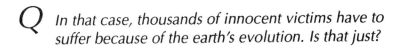

Q *In that case, thousands of innocent victims have to suffer because of the earth's evolution. Is that just?*

I DO not see that what you call death is a disaster. To me, it is the great hour of freedom for the soul.

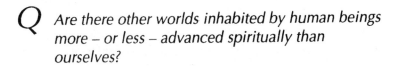

Q *Do you mean that all the people killed in earthquakes are at that particular stage where they are ready for death?*

YES, but they are there because of what has happened in their past lives in your world.

Q *Are there other worlds inhabited by human beings more – or less – advanced spiritually than ourselves?*

OH, yes. There are plenty of worlds inhabited by those who are in advance of your world of matter. This planet you call earth is only one of many planets in the vast universe. There is one planet less spiritually advanced than you.

Q *Why is it that sometimes we want to follow a line of our work that we think is important and we find continual obstruction to our plans?*

ALL the things that are worth doing and worth achieving are those that are the most difficult to perform. The path of attainment is not an easy one. It is full of difficulties, of obstructions, of hamperings that come in the way. Those things are part of the building of character, so that the way you face your difficulties determines the growth of your soul. If you could allow the highest that is within you to express itself without difficulty, it would have little value.

Do not despair. Remember there is no difficulty or obstacle that crosses your path that is so strong that you cannot overcome it by the use of the latent powers that you have within you. Even the difficulties that others place in your path can be swept aside if you will but allow all that is within you to rise and become the master. Your world does not understand that you express so little of yourself while you are in the world of matter.

Q *Of what use is the earth life of all the countless millions of human babies who perish at, or soon after, birth by infanticide or otherwise?*

AS long as people judge eternal principles by material standards they will never understand these things. The wisest of your wise do not see beyond earthly knowledge. When the light of spiritual knowledge reaches them through their evolution, then they will see the Plan which is, as yet, not revealed to them. They see through a glass darkly, and so they do not understand.

Would you attempt to judge the life of a schoolboy only by the years that he goes to school, and ignore that greater life which starts beyond his school? There is a greater life than the one in which you live – a world of beauty, a world of colour, a world of love, a world of labour, a world where every sincere desire finds expression, where every creative impulse can express itself, where everything that cannot be fulfilled in your world is able to realise itself. Until you have seen this world, you cannot criticise the Great Spirit.

Q *Those high spirits with whom you take counsel, do they sometimes come here?*

NO. They are all links in a great chain. As my medium is a link between you and me, and I am a link between you and those beyond me, so they are links between me and those who are beyond them. So it stretches into the inner realms of spirit, much further than my eyes can reach.

Q *Will we ever reach the very highest of all?*

NO. You do not understand. In your world, you can only manifest a small portion of yourself. You cannot express the whole of your soul because it does not yet possess a vehicle of expression. The more I go back into the inner spheres, the more I express of that which is me. That is why we go back at Christmas and Easter, to get something of our real individuality.

You are all children of evolution. That is why you mourn. You should remember that those you love go to express more of themselves in my world.

Q *But why do they go so soon sometimes? It seems they could not have learned their lessons.*

THEY leave your world because a law has been broken. It is only through the bitter crucible of experience that the children of earth will learn, in time, the lessons of the Great Spirit.

If it were all easy, then man would not want to work out his own salvation. Then, in a few generations, you would have nothing in your world through which the Great Spirit could manifest. The soul that goes through the agony of pain, illness, bitterness and sorrow, comes out a greater soul, a soul that understands the sufferings of others.

The soul that lives only in its own butterfly happiness and chases always the illusion and the shadow, one day must learn to touch reality. Do not envy those who you think have an easy time. The hardest road in their life is yet before them. The children of earth must go through every experience, either in your world or mine.

There is a lesson to be learned in everything. You do not reach out and create a vehicle in which to enter that inner perfection until you have emerged triumphant from every experience.

It is hard. Why should it not be hard? Should it be easy to become a saint or a martyr, to be a leader or to be a reformer? Why should it be? The soul that seeks to escape responsibility is not worthy of leading.

Let me say categorically that evolution, physical, mental and spiritual, is a part of the operation of natural law.

The law of evolution embraces every facet of life: insects, birds, fish, humans. They all have their parts to play and are related to one another. No aspect of life is isolated, every form of life is integrated so that the totality forms a composite whole. You are part of the same law of evolution that is responsible for how animals progress.

If you work with the natural laws, if you are in harmony with them, you not only fulfil yourself but at the same time you help the evolution of all other aspects of nature. The whole scheme is divinely ordered so that you play your part as cooperative elements in it. Those who violate nature instead of working with it are performing a disservice to what they violate, and to themselves. Those who cooperate with nature are helping its growth and also helping the unfoldment of their spiritual natures.

Evolution is not a straight line. It is a spiral. At the top things look beautiful, at the bottom they do not look so beautiful.

When I speak of spheres I do not necessarily mean round worlds. I mean planes of being, each graduating into the other, not separated geographically, from the lowest to the highest. It is an infinite evolution.

There is no summit to be attained. As the spirit unfolds, so it is realised there is more to be achieved. It is like knowledge. The more you have, the more you realise there is further knowledge to be gained.

The sphere or plane on which you exist in our world contains individuals at the same stage of spiritual development as you are. You can't go higher spiritually until you are ready. You can go lower, as many of us do in order to perform missionary work among the unenlightened beings in the lower spheres.

Progress consists of shedding imperfections and striving and growing towards perfection all the time.

Destiny

 To what extent does destiny play its part in man's earth life? Could you describe destiny? Is predestination an outside force or your own choice? If you accept reincarnation, can you say why and what purpose it serves?

IT could be both. An outside force helped you to make the choice. You can have free will and destiny at the same time. If you are content to accept that earthly life is the sum total of physical existence, then so be it. But it is conceivable that the spirit which inhabits your present earthly body has existed before, with not necessarily that facet of spirit. It could be that you are a fragment of a very large diamond, with each facet incarnated at differing epochs to make their contribution to the whole.

Q Has the mechanical age helped evolution?

IN the end it does help. You must see evolution as something which is not a straight line. It is a series of advances and retreats. Man rises and falls, man struggles to rise again and rise higher than he fell, and so gradually the race evolves. You can point to epochs and say, "Look! That is a dark stain in evolution". But that is not the whole story; it is but a part of it.

The human spirit is gradually evolving, and with that evolution there comes the obvious lesson that is learned as more and more understand the nature of their own beings, as more and more realise their own possibilities, as more and more know the plan of existence and strive to fit themselves into it.

Centuries ago there were but a handful who dreamed dreams and saw visions. Now the vision splendid has come to hundreds of thousands, and there are countless numbers of reformers, pioneers, teachers, all at work because they know what could be and they desire to help to achieve it. That is where the growth has been made.

Do you think that the latent powers of the soul, infinite in their possibilities of expression, could realise themselves without difficulty and pain, without shadow, without sorrow, and without suffering and misery? Of course not.

The joy and the laughter can only be enjoyed to the full when once you have drained the cup of sorrow to the dregs, for as low as you can fall in the scale of life so correspondingly can you rise. The more you have tasted and experienced that which seems the shadow of earthly life, the more you will appreciate, because of it, the greater joys of the sunshine.

Your experiences are all part of your evolution. One day, freed from the trammels of flesh, with eyes not clouded by matter, you will look back in retrospect and view the life you have lived on earth. And out of the jigsaw of all the events, you will see how every piece fits into its allotted place, how every experience was a lesson to quicken the soul and to enable it to have a greater understanding of its possibilities.

There is no experience which comes to the human soul, which rightly understood and rightly faced, does not leave you better for it. Can you contemplate a world of matter where there were no difficulties, no troubles, no pain, no suffering? There would be nothing to surmount. You would decay.

 Is the development of psychic faculties the next step in man's evolutionary progress?

WITHOUT question, those who are termed psychic, or mediumistic, are the precursors of evolution. They are the advance guard of the next rung in the ladder of evolution. In time to come, psychic faculties will be part of the normal equipment of human beings. Your world is going through a stage of mental unfoldment, and that is why unfolding psychic faculty will follow in its trail.

You must appreciate that man is not an animal confined to five avenues for his sole contacts with the universe, these five windows allow him to know only a small part of universal activity. They limit him to that which can be registered in terms of matter. Man is more than matter, man is mind and spirit, and there are vibrations that belong to the mental and spiritual life. In addition, there are vibrations which belong to the superphysical life, the life that is beyond the earthly world. Man can register the vibrations of this life in which he lives, and the vibrations of that larger life which one day will be his eternal habitat.

 As the majority of Spiritualist churches are situated around London, doesn't it follow that the people here are more highly evolved?

IT does not follow that you are more evolved because you are what is called a 'Spiritualist'. Your evolution depends upon your life, not upon your label. You cannot cheat the laws of the Great Spirit. You obtain growth by growing, evolution by evolving. Character is what you have made it. It is not the profession, the word, the label, the party, the church, the book – these are the trappings. It is what you are that counts and what you do with your life. That applies to all people, and none is outside the law of progress. There is no special prerogative vested in any church, in any place of worship, in the followers of any creed. There are no spiritual privileges obtained by being members of any churches. The only privileges of the spirit that you can have are the ones that you have evolved by the way you have lived your life.

Love

Q   Can you give a definition of love?

LOVE takes many forms, ranging from friendship founded on sympathetic attraction, and mutual interest to the supreme heights where, without thought of self, it seeks to serve wherever it can.

There is a great power in the universe which has never been subject to the analytical scrutiny of laboratories, which cannot be resolved by chemicals or scalpels, yet it is so real that it transcends all other forces which have been measured and weighed and dissected. That love is deathless because it is part of the Great Spirit, the creative spirit of all life, part of the power that has fashioned life; it is indeed the very breath and the very essence of life. And wherever life exists, sooner or later those who are united by its willing bonds will find one another again despite all the handicaps and obstacles and impediments that may be in the way.

First let us be clear: the real love is the love of selflessness; the love that seeks nothing for itself, and in its highest form embraces the whole of humanity. You are not an evolved soul until you can say, because you believe it, "I love all mankind".

That is an ideal, and your world is a long way from it. But there is the love, the undeniable love, between man and woman who are complementary to one another, that is, they are two in form, but one in purpose – they harmonise, they are indeed, as your poet has expressed it, "Two hearts that beat as one". Now, where that love has found itself, there is never any separation. Those whom the law has joined by love can never be sundered in your world or mine.

Where there is that love, and here I am afraid I am going to be controversial, it is always reciprocated. There are aspects of affection, devotion, the desire to serve, maternal instincts, which are believed to be love, but the real love, that only comes once to each man or woman, whether on earth or in the world of spirit, is always reciprocal. The problem does not arise, for in our world, in the fullness of time, each finds the half of its own being.

 How would you interpret the words "the love of the Great Spirit" and "to love our neighbours as ourselves"?

I WOULD interpret both very simply, by saying – live a life of service, forgetting self, try to help wherever you can to raise those who are fallen, drive out all iniquity, and by your own life prove that you are worthy or your divine heritage.

Patriotism and love of the selfish kind

THE motive is the all important qualification. If patriotism means only love of one's country and the people who dwell in it, and there is no wish to extend that love to other countries and other people, then that is a form of selfishness.

The supreme guiding principle is love which expresses itself in service, compassion, humility, tolerance and co-operation, seeking harmony wherever it can. Love is the greatest power in the universe.

Mediumship

Q *Mediums – must they be born or can they be trained?*

YOU must have the gift; it is bestowed on you. Potentially all are mediums in the sense that, being spiritual beings, they have the attributes of the spirit.

Q *Is it necessary for a medium to be deeply entranced for a guide or control to come through?*

NOT at all. It is quite possible for controls and guides to speak through instruments without their being deeply entranced. The great value of the trance state is that it enables the guide or control to have a greater mastery over the make-up of the medium. And the more you succeed in stilling the consciousness of the instrument, the easier the task becomes; but it is not essential to speaking on the part of the control or guide for the medium to be entranced.

Q *Could you give us some advice on what changes should be made in the presentation of mediumship and Spiritualism?*

THERE are new aspects emerging all the time. The physical aspects of mediumship are gradually receding and the higher aspects of healing and teaching are gradually emerging because of a different cycle of evolution in your world. Just go as you are inspired. There are no cut-and-dried formulas for spiritual attainment. You must allow yourself to be led by the same power which has brought you where you are now. It has not failed you. It has brought you here where you are in possession of priceless knowledge which is more important than all your world's material possessions. Just go forward, do the best you can, and you will be guided and sustained.

Lack of mediums

YOU ask about the lack of mediums. There are sufficient mediums for the services that are to be performed at this stage of your evolution. As people are ready to receive, so more mediums will be provided.

They will not necessarily come within the purview of any organisation. They may be in home circles, or individuals working on their own. They may not even call themselves Spiritualists, mediums, psychics or even sensitives. But the label does not matter, the service is important.

Q Is a medium's health affected by trance mediumship?

IT should not be affected in any way except for the better, if he is used according to the known laws that regulate trance mediumship. Obviously, if a trance medium were to allow the situation to get out of hand by indulging in too many sittings, for example, three or four each day, then it might have some adverse effect on his health. But if the sittings follow the normal course, if there are one or two over stated periods and the instrument has been wisely developed, then the result must be an increase in the health of the medium, because the power of the spirit constantly streaming through earthly instruments is one that is so vitalising that it leaves a regenerative effect. Wisely used, all mediumship will improve the health; unwisely used, it will act as a deterrent.

Q Do our spirit friends hear us at all times when we mentally speak to them?

NO, they do not. It depends on whether they are attuned to you. They can hear you if they are in tune. Wherever there is kinship between souls in two states of life, then all the thoughts, all the requests, are immediately known.

Q *Is it now becoming easier for the spirit world to communicate?*

YES, the chaos is gradually being disintegrated and order is coming out of the chaos. The intense and violent emotions are beginning to recede and to dissipate. Slowly, that thick fog which surrounded your earth is breaking up and it is becoming easier to get closer to you, and you will find that this progress will continue.

Q *Why is it that mediums do not always receive surnames in giving clairvoyance?*

BECAUSE, usually, they are more difficult to receive than the other kind. It is all a question of the registration of vibration of sounds. Sounds with which they are already acquainted are easier to be transmitted and received. The more unusual and uncommon the name, the harder it is for it to be transmitted and received. Then again, so much of that which comes from our world is received by mediums in pictorial or symbolic form and often surnames are almost impossible to transmit in terms of pictures of symbols. But where you have instruments who can see very clearly or hear very clearly, they can succeed in registering surnames. It must be remembered that the acid test of mediumship is not the ability to receive surnames, but the ability to give evidence of discarnate presence.

Q *What are the duties of circle doorkeepers?*

THE function of the doorkeeper, is to be the doorkeeper. But he cannot exercise that function until he has sufficient power from you to be able to erect the necessary barriers to keep out those whom he wants to keep out. Do you not understand that the power has to come from you, and that power is a collective power? It is a power which is drawn from each of the sitters and moulded by the guide in charge. Thus it can be used for the purpose of the gathering once those on our side have mixed it and added their own powers to what you have already given.

Spirit communication – its purpose

OUR work is to give that which has a purpose, a significance, so that, while it demonstrates the existence of law, it also enables comfort to be given and knowledge to be spread. Our work is not only to reveal the existence of laws beyond the physical but to reveal the truths of the spirit.

We have a gigantic system of misrepresentation to oppose. We have to undo the work of centuries. We have to destroy the superstructure of falsity that has been built upon the foundations of creeds.

We are striving always to teach the children of matter how to be free and how to bask in the sunlight of spiritual truth, how to cast of the surfdom of creedal slavery. That is not an easy task, for once the trappings of religion have mastered you, it takes a long time for spiritual truth to penetrate that thick wall of superstition.

We strive always to reveal the religious significance of the spiritual truth, for when your world understands its spiritual import there will be a revolution mightier than all the revolutions of war and blood.

It will be a revolution of the soul and, all over the world, people will claim what is their due – the right to enjoy to the full the liberties of the spirit. Away will go every restriction that has put fetters on them.

Our allegiance is not to a creed, not to a book, not to a church, but to the Great Spirit of life and to His eternal natural laws.

 Has there ever been as good communication between the spirit world and this earth as there has been through Spiritualism?

IT has been in bursts of inspiration which have been occasional but not sustained. Now it is organised, harnessed, controlled, regulated. It is all part of one vast plan, a plan that is far more co-ordinated than you can ever realise. The organisation that is behind communication is massive and worked out in masterly detail. It has all been arranged. When it was decided to open the doors of the spirit world it was done deliberately, so that once the doors were opened they could never be closed again.

Service through mediumship

YOU have the inestimable privilege of giving a service that nobody else, not being similarly gifted, can render in your world. Your heart should rejoice to overflowing at the wonderful opportunities presented to you almost daily.

But remember that knowledge always brings responsibility. Never forget that you are entrusted not only with a sublime truth, but with a sublime power, a divine power, the power of life itself, with all that it possesses.

To help regenerate and vitalise is a great responsibility. You will not be led astray, you will always be shown the way. Go forth. Each day brings you wonderful opportunities to serve that should enable you to have an exhilaration of spirit.

Religion

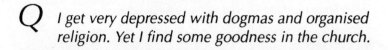 *I get very depressed with dogmas and organised religion. Yet I find some goodness in the church.*

LET us begin at the beginning. Your church, like every other church, temple, synagogue and chapel, owes its existence to the fact that in days gone by the power of the spirit descended in your world. It was accompanied by what are called signs and wonders and sometimes miracles. The power of the spirit came as a challenge to the beliefs, the doctrines, the dogmas of that day. The power of the spirit gave evidence of its divine origin in that its beneficence was demonstrated in healing the sick, in giving guidance and in stressing the fundamental principles of life that matter is a shell and spirit the reality. But alas, the pages of your history show that all such outpourings lasted for only a short while.

Gradually the theologians took control and the mind of man devised teachings which replaced revelations that were divine. Sterility superseded revelation. Again and again there have been some outpourings of the spirit accompanied by signs and wonders and what were believed miracles. And the process was constantly repeated.

 Would you define what you mean by religious tolerance? Cannot your teachings be called dogmatic and intolerant, that the universe is controlled by natural law, that this law is perfect and immutable?

I HAVE never made any claim to infallibility. I am a human being like you, expressing truths which should appeal to your reason. There is no implicit threat that if you reject them you will be subject to any punishment. All we say is that this is truth and we have found it. We offer it to you for your examination. If it measures up to that strict examination accept it; if not, reject it. How else shall we win, with offers of reward or punishment? No, we must win by love, by common sense and by finding that we can meet on common ground.

 Is your philosophy for the masses? Would it not be better for them to have some of the simpler forms of religion, such as the earlier Christians taught, for example, the doctrines of redemption? Is not that doctrine more useful today rather than some of the teachings that people like yourself give?

I WOULD deny the very basis of the question. I affirm that the teachings of the spirit is for the multitude. I assert that it is the simple truth which the multitude can understand, assimilate and prize, and that it will provide them with all that they require in the name of religion. The test of all teaching is simple – is it true? No other standard matters. The other teachings to which reference has been made have failed to gain increasing support because they are not true. An instance is offered of the belief in redemption. None can redeem you; you must redeem yourself. None can bear upon his shoulders the responsibilities of your life. None can absolve you from the sins that you have committed. None can interfere or alter the law of cause and effect which operates with inexorable precision.

 Is it desirable that there should be a fusion of what we know as Spiritualism and orthodoxy?

ALL this is but a question of words. I am not interested in titles, labels and classifications. I am interested in the spread of truth. Whatever helps to spread truth, to free mankind, to equip the children of the Great Spirit for the life that awaits them and enables them to live, worthy of their divine heritage, while they are on earth – whatever achieves that has my blessing and the blessing of every enfranchised soul. I am not concerned with what is called Spiritualism or what is called orthodoxy, for these terms are too general and their classification leads to confusion. I am concerned with individuals striving to find light, seeking to unfold their innate divinity so that they can help all those who are less fortunate than themselves. It is enough for every individual to do the best they can with the gifts that he possesses and to know day by day that he has served the Great Spirit and His children to the best of his ability.

Bible

 Is there a lot of truth in the Bible?

IT is a mixture of divine truth and man's falsification.

Orthodoxy

Iniquity of Orthodoxy

Q Why are so many of the lives, deaths and resurrections of figureheads of religion, including the Christian religion, similar to those of the mythological gods whose lives were based on the phenomena of nature, such as the solar system and the seasons?

IT is because the children of earth have always borrowed from the myths of ancient times in order to invest their leaders with supernatural powers. They did not understand the operation of natural laws. They wanted the one whom they considered to be the greatest of all to be endowed with attributes beyond the reach of the other children of the Great Spirit. And so they have borrowed from one another. But that does not affect the teaching which was given by the messengers of the Great Spirit who, each in his own day, reflected some of the truth, wisdom and love of the Great Spirit.

Q Is it an accident that these lives do, according to their followers, follow the course of nature, many of the recorded incidents in their lives being suggestive of natural law, such as resurrection following death as the spring follows winter?

IF you mean the story in the Bible that, when the Nazarene was crucified, there was great thunder and lightning, that is not true. If you mean that all those who die, as your world calls it, return, that is true. I understand the question to refer to the additions to the historical lives of the messengers of the Great Spirit.

Q *What is the sin against the Holy Ghost?*

THE sin against the Holy Ghost is to deny the Holy Ghost.

Q *What is the Holy Ghost?*

IT is the power of the spirit which descends in to the world of matter. Your churches worship it in the abstract, but they reject it when it descends on millions all over the world, for it is that power which we use to commune with you. It is that power of the Great Spirit which enables, even for a short time, the world of spirit and the world of matter to become one in harmony of purpose.

Q *I have been told that baptism in any denomination has, as its object, that when a spirit passes over, a band of spirits belonging to that denomination receive it and care for it until it is adjusted to the new conditions. If this is so, what happens to non-baptised souls?*

THE power that set the universe in motion, the Spirit that breathed into a body the breath of life and made it a living soul, the Great Spirit Who is responsible for all the worlds, for all the laws of the universe, the Great Spirit who is expressed in life in all its varying degrees, the Great Spirit Who has been revealed throughout all the ages by all the seers and the instruments, the Great Spirit Who is within all, the Great Spirit Who is behind all, is not troubled whether a man has sprinkled water or not.

What does matter is whether the life has been lived in accordance with his highest ideals. The laws cannot be cheated because a few drops of water are sprinkled on a baby. The laws cannot be altered, for effect always follows cause.

Q *Has not Christianity produced plenty of good men?*

THEY would have been good just the same, whether they were Christians or not.

Q *But are not some good because they try to follow the teachings of Jesus?*

WHEN your world emulates the Nazarene, a new chapter will have begun in history. It has not happened yet. I do not see any signs of it. Do not speak to me of "Christians", whose lives mock the one they profess to serve. Did not the Nazarene say: "Not every one that saith unto me, Lord, Lord, shall enter the kingdom of heaven; but he that doeth the will of my Father is in heaven"?

Q *Are there not thousands of Christians who believe the creeds superficially and who yet live very good lives and who are unselfish?*

THEY are not good Christians. They are bad Christians, but good men. Remember this, every creed fetters the soul. Men are not good because of creed, but in spite of creed. In the name of creed they have killed one another and they have burned one another. Anything which binds, which cramps the soul, which prevents it from having full expression, must be swept away.

Q *Was Jesus Christ "God the Son", as the Church says, or was he an ordinary man with great mediumistic powers?*

THE Nazarene was a messenger of the Great Spirit who came into your world of matter in order to fulfil a mission of the Great Spirit. He fulfilled his mission on earth, but he has not yet fulfilled the rest of his mission, which is still being directed from the world of spirit. It is wrong to worship the Nazarene, for worship should be given only to the Great Spirit and not to His messengers. The Nazarene came into your world by fulfilling the natural laws which the Great Spirit had ordained, the same natural laws which all must fulfil in order to be born into your world. You cannot live, you cannot be born into your world, you cannot pass from your world into mine, except through the natural laws of the Great Spirit.

Q   *Can you substantiate that by reference to the Bible texts?*

MY appeal is only to the laws of the Great Spirit. Those who rely on the crutches of words must be left until their souls can be awakened to an understanding that the Great Spirit is still at work, still inspiring, still revealing.

His laws are still in operation and His power can flow through instruments today, if they will allow themselves to be used for the Great Spirit, as instruments were used many, many years ago. The Bible, as you call it, is a great book. But there is a greater Bible. It is the universe, which is sustained by the laws of the Great Spirit. From that, you can learn far more than from any book in your world of matter, however great it may be, however respected it may be, however revered it may be.

Q   *Where is Jesus now and what is he doing?*

THE spirit that worked through the Nazarene is still at work, seeking to continue the work that it started two thousand years ago, but that spirit has been crucified a thousand times since, and is being crucified almost every day. But, because that spirit is part of the Great Spirit, it will continue to spread its influence wherever there are instruments who can work for the Great Spirit to bring peace and happiness to your world of matter.

When you speak of the Nazarene, do you mean the man Jesus or the spirit forces working through him?

THE man. But he has since evolved and there is now a far greater spiritual consciousness expressed through him than there was in the earthly incarnation, for the amount that he expressed then had to be in consonance with the limitations of his day. There has never been on earth anyone through whom the manifestation of the spirit has been greater than through the Nazarene. There has never been any through whom the laws have revealed themselves at so great an intensity as the Nazarene.

 Not in two thousand years?

NO, neither before nor since. That was the greatest manifestation of the Great Spirit that your world has yet received. But we do not rever the man as he incarnated on earth. We pay tribute to the power which operated through him. We recognise that the man is only entitled to respect in so far as he was the instrument for the power of the spirit.

Q Is the spirit world planning a further revelation by sending another teacher like Jesus?

DIFFERENT methods are being used to suit the different needs. You must remember that your world has become more complex, more interdependent, and more channels of communication have had to be opened. We have to meet with different temperaments and different habits, thoughts, ways and modes of life. Our message has to be adapted to national environments and characteristics, to racial habits. It has to be given in the language and the limitations of a variety of people. But behind the focus of the power is the same driving force.

Your Christian world pays its tribute to one who rose from the "dead", who was seen after his "death", who demonstrated that life continues beyond "death". The Nazarene demonstrated that he was the same individual and he gave as proofs, in the materialised body, the earthly marks of the crucifixion. After that, he revealed himself again.

Your Christian world believes that; though it cannot prove it. But it says it was a miracle! We have returned through the same laws to demonstrate the life beyond death, to show that the Great Spirit is eternal and the operation of His laws immutable, that even as one was resurrected so are all resurrected, because resurrection is a law of the Great Spirit of life.

Creeds v Truth

[IT took twenty-five theologians fifteen years to produce "Doctrine in the Church of England", in January 1938, Silver Birch was asked to comment on some extracts which were read to him]:

"The Resurrection of Jesus is an act of God wholly unique in human history."

DID it take fifteen years to arrive at that conclusion? How true it is that those who betray the Nazarene are those who call themselves Christians!

Resurrection is part of the law of life. Resurrection comes to every soul when it is resurrected from the body of matter when death arrives. Resurrection belongs to no one man. It belongs to all the children of the Great Spirit, for everyone in turn must pass through the portal of death, leaving behind the body of matter, and begin a new life in the realm of spirit, in the body of spirit, which has been preparing itself all the time. The Nazarene did nothing contrary to the natural law. He came to fulfil the law, and all his actions and all his teachings were part of the Law.

Did he not say: "All these things shall ye do and greater things than these shall ye do"? If you elevate the Nazarene to so remote and inaccessible a place in the high heavens that no child of the Great Spirit can reach him, then you have destroyed the whole value of his mission, for the essence of the Nazarene's life was to demonstrate what could be achieved by all the children of the Great Spirit if they would but allow the fullness of the Great Spirit to reveal itself in their lives. And when he passed to the world of spirit he returned, as many before him and as countless thousands have returned since. There is nothing unique in the universe, for the laws of the Great Spirit are always in operation, and the mere fact that anything has ever happened is proof of the existence of law.

"Baptism, even infant baptism, is a means of   deliverance from the domination of influences which predispose to sin. In the life of the unbaptised saint there is a defect."

NO priest possesses the power of magic, to make water anything but water. Because a priest takes drops of water and sprinkles it on the brow of a child, he does not in any way do anything which affects the child's life in your world or mine. These drops of water were drops of water before and they were drops of water afterwards. The priest has no power to change their chemical constituents and to make them do something which is contrary to the law.

The soul is unaffected by baptism, for none has the power to evolve your soul for you. That you must do yourself, by the quality of the life that you live in the world of matter. The effects of your actions cannot be removed by any other, but only by the compensation that you make and the retribution that you have to suffer.

Saintliness has nothing whatsoever to do with baptism. Saintliness consists of allowing the Great Spirit to shine through your life, so that you achieve as much of perfection in daily life as you can reach whilst you are in the world of matter.

"God could work miracles if he pleased, but the commission is divided as to whether or not miraculous events occur."

WOULD they have been sure if they had deliberated for another fifteen years? How piteous a spectacle, the blind leading the blind! These are your teachers and they cannot tell you whether or not these things happened! There are no miracle. There have never been any miracles. There never will be miracles. The Great Spirit is the Great Spirit, and the laws of the Great Spirit are perfect in their operation. They were conceived by Perfection. If the Great Spirit has to suspend the laws that perfection created, then chaos must result. If the Great Spirit has to interfere in the scheme of creation to provide for events which he has not foreseen, then the Great Spirit ceases to be Perfection. The Great Spirit becomes imperfect.

If the Great Spirit has to perform a miracle to bestow favours on some, then the Great Spirit is a partial deity and not the Infinite Spirit of all life. Because they are ignorant of the higher laws, because they do not know the power of the spirit, because they themselves are not touched by the power which comes from our realms, they cannot understand these happenings wrought through mediums. Because they seem to think that events of the days of the Nazarene contradict what is known today of the physical laws, they are compelled to think of miracles. Yet, if they understood the operation of the laws of the spirit, they would see that the Great Spirit is the same yesterday, today and forever, and that His power is available and accessible to all who enable His gifts to be exercised in their lives.

"A miracle, if it occurs, is not a breach of order, but expresses the purpose of God, which also determines the order of nature. It is therefore nothing irrational or capricious."

THEY do not understand that all the laws of the Great Spirit have always been in existence; will always be in existence. You only discover in your world of matter the operation of laws because through your inventions you are enabled to register some of the more subtle phases of universal life. But you have not created anything. You have only discovered that which always was in existence. It is impossible for something new to be created, for all that is part of creation already exists. Nothing can happen to contradict the laws of the Great Spirit, for all the laws already exist, whether you know of their existence or not.

It is not necessary for the Great Spirit to create new laws, for all the laws are in existence. All that is necessary for the universe is here now, always has been, always will be. The Great Spirit, being perfect, has foreseen all that is needed in every stage of existence.

"From the Christian standpoint the Bible is unique, as being the inspired record of a unique revelation."

HOW dark are their minds! How they are engulfed in the inky blackness of superstition! How thick is the wall that surrounds them! How deeply they have entrenched themselves behind the fortress of superstition!

Ever since your world of matter has been the world of matter, teachers have come to reveal the Great Spirit to his children. They have spoken the language of the day. The revelation was adapted to the demands of their day, to the country in which they lived, to the stage of growth and development of people. It had to be given in such a manner as it was capable of being understood – not too high, so as to be beyond their reach.

But always the process of evolution has been at work and, as the children of the Great Spirit have evolved and grown, so new teachers arose, new seers, new prophets and new visionaries, each with his vision, his dreams, his prophecies, his message, his inspiration, his truth, his teaching adapted to the needs of his day. There is no finality in revelation, for the Great Spirit is perfect.

The revelation of today is in line with the revelation of yesterday. We do not deny the truths taught by the Nazarene. The Nazarene did not deny the truths taught by Moses. And those who will come after us, in the world of your tomorrow, will not deny the truths taught by us today. But, because the children of tomorrow will be at a higher stage of evolution, the truth that is to be revealed to them must be more progressive than the truth that is revealed to you today.

"For him (the Christian), Christ is the one, and the necessary mediator. Christ's access to the Father was direct, we have our access to the Father through him."

NO. The Great Spirit is within you. You are in the Great Spirit. "The Kingdom of Heaven is within", taught the Nazarene. How little they know of their own Christian teachings! You are never separated from the Great Spirit. The Great Spirit is never separated from you. There is nothing you can ever do, no vile crime that you can commit of so degrading an intensity that can ever cut you off from the Great Spirit. The tie that binds you to the Great Spirit is imperishable and therefore you can never be lost.

You approach the Great Spirit direct, as you learn to allow the Great Spirit to express Himself in your lives. Each one of you has a portion of the Great Spirit and you require nobody to stand between you and the Great Spirit of life.

That was not the purpose of the Nazarene. He came to teach the people how to live their lives, that the fullness of the Great Spirit may be expressed.

Theology is the curse of the world of matter. It puts mankind in shackles. It puts his soul in prison. To be freed, he must learn to sever himself from all limiting creeds and restrictive dogmas and to find the unfettered truth that comes in spiritual inspiration. The mind of man cannot exceed the inspiration of the Great Spirit.

"The resurrection confirms man's hope of immortality."

SO much to learn! So much to learn! You live because you have part of the Great Spirit within you. Matter only exists because of spirit. Spirit is the eternal reality. Spirit is indestructible, imperishable, immortal, infinite. You will live beyond the grave, beyond the fire of creation, because you are spirit. Nothing in the world of matter, nothing in the realms of spirit, can destroy the imperishable divinity which is yours, the gift of life conferred on you by your entry into this world.

Because you are a spirit, you live. Because you are a spirit you survive the grave. Because you are a spirit you will continue to live forever and forever. It has nothing to do with any teacher. It is part of your birthright, part of your heritage. They would seek to limit the Great Spirit, the Divine Architect, the Power which maintains the whole universe in all its multitudinous expressions – to what? To one being who lived for thirty-three years in the world of matter. And they would seek to restrict His bounty to those who espouse a creed. Oh no! They shame the meaning of the word "religion". Did they but know it, they make the Nazarene weep tears of bitterness and sorrow, and they continue to crucify him.

You are not the salt of the earth because you call yourselves Christians. You are not the salt of the earth because you belong to a Church. You will not be judged in my world by the label you have worn on earth. Your championship of a creed will not matter. All that will be of any account is one thing – how much of the Great Spirit you have expressed whilst you were on earth.

"Fundamental to the Christian doctrine of the Atonement is the conviction that it is essentially the work of God, who, in Christ, reconciles mankind to Himself."

IS this a repetition of the old teaching of the atonement? Does it mean that a jealous and angry god had to be appeased by the blood sacrifice of the one he loved? Does it mean that the Great Spirit is more cruel and more heartless than an angry human being? Does it mean that the Great Spirit demands blood to be shed to reconcile Himself with His children? How pitiable a conception is this of the Great Spirit and of the mission of the Nazarene! He was full of the love and mercy and gentleness of a loving Father. You are all placed in the world of matter to build your own characters and accomplish your own soul evolution.

If you choose the path of selfishness you must pay the price. If you choose the path of service, you receive the reward that comes in the growth of character. It is all fixed by the operation of law, and not even the greatest of the great teachers can alter the operation of those laws.

All else is a doctrine of cowardice and injustice. If you have done wrong, be a man and pay the price! Do not attempt to shelve your responsibilities on to the back of another. In our world, the saint, the altruist, has reached a higher level than the selfish man because his soul has grown much more. How else could it be? Could one man be selfish and reach, after what you call death, the same level as he who devoted his whole life to service? Is it thus that you would mock the Great Spirit and His perfect justice? Of course not. Life is what you make it. No matter what your sphere, no matter what your occupation, whether you be born of high or low parentage, whatever your rank or title your colour or race or nationality, you all have opportunities for service. If you neglect them you pay the price, and none can interfere. Let me finish by quoting the words of the Nazarene: "That which a man sows he must reap".

Attitude to Orthodoxy

Q When dealing with the orthodox is it better to be gentle or harsh?

SPEAK the truth, fear no man. You are a servant of the Great Spirit. Always refute evil, always answer lies. Be fearless.

Spiritualism

Q Should people put orthodox religion behind them when they accept the tenets of Spiritualism?

I AM not bothered with these labels, I am not sure whether I am a Spiritualist, because I have not been confirmed. What you call yourself does not matter. We are concerned with the way you live your life. Religion, what is it? Is it going to church, synagogue, chapel or temple? Is it the acceptance of certain theological ideas devised by man? Is it calling yourself a Roman

Catholic, a Protestant, a Buddhist, a Jew? Religion is living in a way that brings you closer to the Great Spirit. Religion is when the Great Spirit is expressed in your actions. Religion is service.

If you find there are some people who have all the benefits of communication with our world but still adhere to certain conventional theological beliefs, then be sorry for them. Say a silent prayer for them because they are still only on the first rungs of the ladder, or are in the halfway stage.

Religious leaders

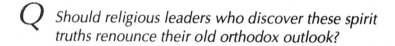

Q *Should religious leaders who discover these spirit truths renounce their old orthodox outlook?*

WE have enshrined personal responsibility as one of the supreme principles. Each soul is responsible for what it does. You cannot equivocate with the truths of the spirit. As awareness comes, so the voice of conscience says what should be done. If it is accepted and recognised then that soul must do what it implies. I will not condemn individuals because it is not right and proper for me to do so.

Q *Will Spiritualism ever become a universal religion?*

WHAT you call Spiritualism is but the name given to certain natural laws, their operation and their implications. To me, religion is the living of life, not the acceptance of certain sectarian beliefs.

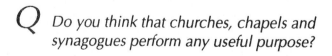

Q *Do you think that churches, chapels and synagogues perform any useful purpose?*

SOME of them do and some of them do not. Where those who are in church are amenable to the influence of the spirit, albeit unconsciously, and they are vessels of inspiration, then they are able to be of great service because they are used to spread light, knowledge, wisdom and truth. Where in these houses of worship there is no inspiration, where sole reliance is placed on ancient formularies, on dead rituals and decayed creeds, where nothing is said except that which conforms to the strict letter of theology, then no service is being rendered. It is impossible to make generalisations, to indulge in sweeping condemnations or to give wholehearted approval. Each must be examined on its merits, by virtue of the service it renders, or fails to render.

HEALING

Healing

Pain

Q *I have just been in touch with a case of cancer.*
The pain is just beginning and it does seem wrong.

BUT pain can be alleviated. There are medical means of doing so. If pain is the problem it can be dealt with. Even when conditions are intolerable I must insist this is not the final verdict so far as we are concerned. I would be false to everything that I teach if I said that the final verdict is to be given by those whose minds are restricted to one set scale of discipline.

Cancer

Q *Do spirit doctors know the cure for cancer?*

THERE is no specific cure in the sense that there is one remedy that will cure every type of cancer, because they do not all owe their origin to the same cause. Some are physical, some are mental and some are spiritual in their origin. It is not possible to treat them all alike. You must try to understand the way we work. It is not done by saying, "Your world has a problem, here is the answer". Your world must earn the answer. But if you have wrong living in your world, if you have the needless cruelty to which helpless animals are subjected, if you have not earned the right to be cured, then no one can give you a cure.

What is done is twofold. Where patently sincere and devoted individuals are working along truly spiritual lines, they are helped automatically because they attract wiser beings who were in their field and who desire to help them. The other method is by the outpouring of spirit power in healing which produces results when the sufferer is ready to receive them. All

76

healing from our world is accomplished through spirit power. It is not a magic wand that can be waved. That power is attracted to the soul of the sufferer. Therefore it cannot induce a response until the soul is touched. There is no magnetic link until the soul is open. If it is closed in, it cannot make any contact. It also depends on other factors, too. It depends on what is the cause of the disease. It depends on the purpose for which that soul is incarnated. It depends whether a choice has been made beforehand to express itself through a certain type of bodily mechanism. It is not a simple question.

Euthanasia

 Why are people left on earth, unable to do anything for themselves, for example after a car accident? Why cannot euthanasia be put into practice?

IT says somewhere in your Bible, "The Lord giveth and the Lord taketh away; blessed be the name of the Lord". I quote these words because they are true. Life comes from the Great Spirit. You cannot create life, neither can you destroy it. You can provide the mechanism in which life will function. You can destroy that mechanism, but the gift of life is not yours. Life is the responsibility which is entrusted to you.

When it comes to judgement, beware of making assessments based only on physical measurements. You cannot measure the spirit with a physical yardstick. Your natural pity, sympathy, mercy and compassion are aroused when you see an individual reduced to what you call a cabbage. But the cabbage has a life and a purpose to serve in your world otherwise it would not be there.

A person is injured in an accident. His body is so mutilated that its machinery is not capable of giving the spirit the fullness of its expression. Do you regard this problem as physical or spiritual? Spiritually there is a purpose to be served, a lesson to be learned, an experience to be undergone. Physically it may all seem motiveless. But until you can see with the eye of the spirit, until you can understand eternal scales of values, your judgements must of necessity be based on fallacies.

I am completely and utterly opposed to killing these individuals, though the act is qualified by the motive for doing so. This, however, is not the answer. Once you entrust to others the decision as to when they shall kill, you are giving them a power they are all not capable of having. Nor should they have the responsibility of this decision.

Q *Can euthanasia ever be right?*

THIS is a question I have answered before – and I am against it. I say no, not because I am indifferent or callous to suffering. You cannot live for long in our world without becoming increasingly sensitive to the pains of others. But I feel that the verdict of determining the end of the manifestation of life through a body should not be placed, generally speaking, in the hands of those who are woefully ignorant of spiritual truths and who are not, unfortunately, experts as to what is and is not curable.

Malformed babies – unfair?

THOSE who talk of unfairness are still thinking in terms of bodies, of a world of matter, and not of an infinite life. The spirit does not suffer from venereal disease. The spirit is not crippled or misshapen or bent. The spirit is not suffering from any hereditary traits or any of the acquired characteristics of the parent. These do not change the individual, although they do affect the body through which the spirit manifests on earth.

Whilst you can quite possibly argue that, from the earthly point of view, looking at life solely from a material standpoint, the one who is born into a diseased body has a much worse time physically than the one born into a healthy body; those opinions do not hold in regard to the spirit which is behind the body. You will not automatically be poorer in spirit because your body is diseased, and the richer in spirit because your body is healthier. Indeed, it can be argued that your spirit will be richer because you will have learned the many lessons of pain and suffering which are all part of the equipment of the spirit in its essential evolution.

Illness – apparent injustices

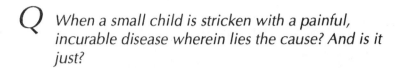

Q When a small child is stricken with a painful, incurable disease wherein lies the cause? And is it just?

YOU will not solve spiritual problems with material measurements. You cannot judge eternity by the portion of it that you experience in your very short earthly life. You cannot comprehend divine justice, which is ruled by infinite laws, when you see only one infinitesimal fragment of life at work. How can the lesser comprehend the greater? How can the drop of water judge the ocean? How can the fragment explain the whole?

The universe is ruled by wondrous laws to which I pay constant tribute, for they were conceived by perfect wisdom. They make no mistakes. Sometimes it will seem to you that there is injustice because you only know part of the story. When you see the whole of the story you will change your opinion. You cannot, whilst in earthly life with its short span, understand infinity. You cannot know anything of compensation or retribution.

You have no means of appreciating the vast richness, beauty and wonder of a spirit life which has no means of offering you any comparisons with what you already know. How then can it be explained to those whose judgements must be limited, whose vision must be restricted, what the other side of the picture is?

If you have children born because the physical apparatus is constructed by the parents, then surely it must be apparent that whatever is in the physical make-up of the parents must go into the child's structure. Thus the sins of the parents are visited on the children. But the child is, by virtue of its birth, a part of the Great Spirit. It has a divine heritage, a latent, infinite divinity that can outweigh all physical disadvantages. Matter is not superior to spirit; matter is the servant; spirit is the master.

Spiritual growth is a slow but certain process. Spiritual perception and understanding can come only when the soul is ready. To some the truths that we have to preach must fall on deaf ears. It was always so. When the soul is touched it will be ready to appreciate truths that are waiting for it. You cannot place yourself in the position of the Great Spirit pronouncing judgement.

Birth – Caesarian and time of

IT alters only the time of entry into your world. It does not alter the time when the spirit has started at the moment of conception to begin to express itself.

Epilepsy

Q Can you tell us what causes someone to become or be an epileptic?

THERE is a disturbance in the brain which makes it impossible for it to register and to have the correct stimuli from the mind of the individual.

Q But can it be cured?

OF course, every disease can be cured. There is no such thing as an incurable disease. There are only people who could be incurable.

Problems of healing

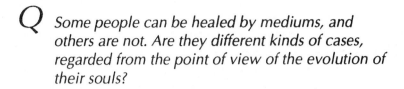

Some people can be healed by mediums, and others are not. Are they different kinds of cases, regarded from the point of view of the evolution of their souls?

NO. If they are to pass into my world, there is no healer in your world who can prevent their passing.

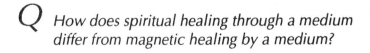

But some who go to healers would otherwise pass on.

A few days, more or less, what are they in eternity?

Q Does not that make healing rather unnecessary?

NO, because to express service is to express the Great Spirit. Much of your sickness and disease is not due to the evolution of the soul, but because, in ignorance, man lives contrary to the law. It is true that he lives contrary to the Law because his soul has not yet reached the state of evolution where he understands the Law. When your soul has so expressed itself in evolution that it is one with the Law, there is no sickness then.

Q How does spiritual healing through a medium differ from magnetic healing by a medium?

THEY are quite different. Magnetic healing is dependent on the radiations of the medium's own psychic powers. Spiritual healing is dependent upon the instrument being attuned to the vibrations of the spirit, so that rays, which are normally beyond the range of the world of matter, can be sent through the medium.

Pain and suffering

PAIN and suffering are regarded as miseries. They are not. They have divine parts to play in the evolution of the individual. What you have to do is to help those that are brought to you. If it is an evolved person, try to comfort the individual with the evidence that can be obtained about the reality of the afterlife: that love, like life, continues to survive.

If it is a sick person, the healing is the demonstration of a power at work for which there is no material explanation. If it is someone who has lost his way, guidance can be provided.

Why some respond and others do not

EVERY happening has its purpose. There are no accidents or coincidences, only planned operations, laws of cause and effect at work.

At some stage in human life the Great Spirit provides his children with an opportunity not only of finding themselves, but of achieving self-realisation. To do so, the soul has to be touched.

Now, if the soul is not touched the power of the spirit cannot work. If a cure is achieved and a soul is not touched, then the healing has failed in its purpose also.

The healing will succeed only when the patient is spiritually ready and touched, because then there is the quickening of the soul. Otherwise it is a purely physical reflex action. Success may be temporary or permanent, but what is vital is the effect on the patient's spiritual nature.

No hope

THE story of every potential healer and medium follows a similar pattern. They reach that stage when they feel that nothing materially offers any hope. It is then that the soul becomes ready to receive the influx of power and inspiration which will enable the owner to begin to fulfil himself or herself.

Cases where healing doesn't work

OF course it is sad, but it is sad for them. You cannot cure them all. There are some who will never be cured in your world. They are paying karmic debts and have lessons to learn. Healing will not touch them. That is why I say do the best you can. You are there to be available. What happens after you have done healing is not your responsibility. You have to provide the best conditions, to be the purest channel. Reach out to the highest you can attain; that is your responsibility. But remember, you are helping souls to find themselves that otherwise would not have done so.

How can a healer help?

YOUR world is full of millions of people who do not know what they are there for, who they are, what it is that they must achieve whilst they are incarnate on earth. You can help them to realise that they are spirits with bodies, that the real individual is the deathless spirit, that the spirit is there to gain the experience to equip it for its larger life in our world. That is the most important thing that you can do.

You demonstrate that the Great Spirit, the apex of love and wisdom and compassion, provides everyone with the opportunity to find himself or herself and begin to live, as all people in your world should live, not in superstition, ignorance or darkness, but in the full light of knowledge, with serenity and confidence as their constant companions.

Helping others

HELP wherever the opportunity arises, and know that you are fulfilling yourself, which is the purpose for your being on earth.

Why do some mediums become ill?

MEDIUMS cannot be exempt from natural law, which encompasses all without exception and without deviation. If there is ill health there are two reasons.

One is that there is not the harmony between spirit, mind and body which produces the wholeness that is health. The other possibility is a karmic condition, which means that the soul has yet to achieve progress on earth that cannot be achieved elsewhere because of what has happened in a previous existence.

In an ideal world mediums would be ideal people, but you are not living in an ideal world.

Ill health in a healer

Q Should a temporary halt be called to healing work if a healer becomes ill?

NO. Only unless they are in such a pitiable condition it makes it impossible for the power of the spirit to operate. There are many excellent healers who suffer from poor health because they are transmitters; as long as they have the power to transmit they will have the power flow through them.

Healing – as part of a plan

 In cases where the patient creates the circumstances continuously which create the illness, is it part of the plan that healing should be given again and again?

WHAT we must do is to help souls who come to us. What they do afterwards is their responsibility. If only the body is made well, then the healing has failed. It is the soul which must be touched and quickened into activity.

If they have not learned the implications as to how they should order their lives as a result of the healing, then that must be accounted a failure. They should realise that the power that has been at work is intended not only to heal bodies, but to heal minds so that there is an understanding of what life is all about. It takes time.

Fulfilment

IF you can help just one soul to find itself, if you comfort only one mourner, if you heal only one sick person, then the whole of your earthly life has been justified. How privileged you are to be aware of the tremendous power that is around and about you, that enfolds you, guards you, directs you and ensures that you will continue to unfold your latent divinity and the gifts which are your cherished possessions.

Becoming a healer

 What happens when you become the channel as a healer?

THE life force, that is, the power of the spirit, pours through you and makes contact with the soul of the patient to charge that battery and establish the harmony which has been disrupted by whatever conditions caused the disease.

The essence of healing is that the healer should have suffered and have compassion for the sufferer who comes to him. It is the only way that the laws work.

 Should a healer be concerned with the same thing time and time again if necessary?

YOU must not be in a position where you refuse to help. A soul asks for help, and it is no part of the healer's province to lay down laws as to how it should be given. The healer's task is to heal. If the sufferer's soul is touched, enlightenment will come. If it is not touched, then at least you have made a body better than it was before, even if only for a short time.

You must do the best you can and never refuse help when it is sought. The healer must be available. If a recipient misbehaves later and induces more difficulties, that is his responsibility.

 When is a soul ready?

AS to what constitutes readiness, the answer is the gold that can only be found after it has gone through the process of eliminating the dross.

If earthly life was a monotone; if there was only light and no darkness, joy and no pain, food and no hunger, you would not appreciate its value. It is life's polarity that brings you an understanding of its purpose and possibilities.

 What would healers need that they have not got now to be able to treat patients by psychic surgery?

YOU must not think in terms only of achieving demonstrable physical results with healing. Healing is primarily a spiritual happening. The object of healing is to touch the soul of the patient. If the patient's soul is ripe, the mind will be right and the body will be right. Thus healing leads to a correct alignment of spirit, mind and body so that they function in harmony. That is what health means: wholeness, harmony.

To remove a growth is not the objective – it is to touch the soul. You can have cancer of the spirit in that sense. Selfishness and all the wrong growths persist within, and until these are eradicated there can be no true spiritual progress. It is the spirit that must be paramount in all life. Until the spirit rules there will never be harmony, health, happiness or the fullness of living.

Passing over after healing

 On three or four occasions when I have been asked to give absent healing I have been unfortunate to be, in my way of thinking, unsuccessful. Each one has passed over.

THIS may be the greatest success you have achieved. If you have helped a soul in its passing, that is a successful healing. The object of healing is not to prolong physical life. It is to touch the spirit. Get your first things first. It is the spirit that matters. If the spirit is right, the body will be right.

Healing and visualisation

Q It has been said that nothing material on our plane manifests but what it is preceded by thought. In other words, we build a thought matrix. Does it help if a healer mentally visualises the perfect healing as he tries to approach his patient and builds the image of perfect health?

IT helps tremendously because your thought is a reality. The more you think of perfect health, the closer you come to attaining it. You should always strive your utmost for the ideal. You should always visualise the best. You should never abandon hope. Always radiate cheer and optimism. These are the conditions in which spirit power produces its best results.

Maintaining health

Q Does tranquillity and attunement to the inner force help us to maintain health?

IT would apply if all men lived their lives in accordance with the natural law, and did nothing to bring about disharmony between mind, body and spirit. The whole mode of earthly life has been based on the supremacy of matter over mind and not mind over matter. The mind is supreme, the spirit is king, but the kingdom depends on your activity.

Q Why are some patients healed and others cannot be?

BECAUSE some are ready to be healed spiritually and others are not. The acid test is not whether the body is healed, but whether the soul is touched.

Q *Why are some people not healed?*

BECAUSE they have not spiritually earned the right to be healed.

Q *That seems to me rather an over-simplification suggesting that if he is a bad person he would never be healed and a good one will always be healed.*

IT is not as simple as that. This is too facile because you have to remember you are not necessarily looking at the problem with the eyes of the spirit. To you, suffering is terrible. To us, it can be divine. To you, disaster is the end. To us, it is sometimes the beginning of a new life. You must not bandy these terms of good and bad as if they are fixed objectives based upon a material evaluation. Our standards of appraisal are not always the same as yours. I say that a person must have spiritually earned the right to be healed. I did not say that he was good or bad. Once the spirit has come into its own, it has earned the right to be healed. The healing will be effective.

Healing and karma

YOU asked about karma, the law of cause and effect, sowing and reaping, which operates in all worlds and at all times. Sometimes you have a patient with a karmic condition which is a carry-over from a previous existence. If the karmic condition has not out-worked itself, the healing will appear to be a failure. If the patient has reached that stage in spiritual development where the effect has completely followed the cause and there is no more karma to manifest, the healing will be successful because the soul is ready.

What makes one person a better healer than another?

THE same thing that makes one person a better speaker than another, a better pianist than another, a better writer than another. The gift is nearer the surface.

Spirit power

 Can you tell us the manner in which that power is created on your side of life, that is, the power that is characterised for particular conditions with people who are ill?

THIS is very difficult because it is hard to find words to describe non-material forces. What you have to try to realise is that spirit power is the life force, the stuff of life itself. It is animation. It is infinite. It is malleable. It can take a myriad different shapes. It is capable of an infinite number of permutations and combinations.

We have people in our world of varying degrees of knowledge, experience and understanding. We have the equivalent of what you would call chemists and scientists, who are forever blending aspects of this life force, this power of the spirit, to characterise it, to use your word, which is a very good one. They are always experimenting so that it can be conditioned to the greatest possible extent through the instrument, who is the channel, and bearing in mind the nature of the complaint or ailment which is to receive the healing. I do not think I can put it any other way.

It is an individual process for every sufferer who comes to the healer. The aura of the patient helps a great deal, because this gives a perfect picture of the spiritual and mental conditions which are responsible for the ailment in the first place, and this determines the blending that has to be done.

Q *Does this require a mental effort on the part of those in the spirit world who are able to do this?*

MENTAL is not the right word, because it is very real; it is an actual blending. We use the spiritual equivalent of what you would call chemicals. The mind has to be used because in our world the mind is the reality for building everything.

Q *Bearing in mind the effort of absent healing, to what extent are we used, either our physical or spirit body, in contact healing for this spirit power?*

BUT you are used in absent healing, too.

Q *Are our physical or spirit bodies used in absent healing, or are we simply used because of our attunement to make the link?*

YOUR spirit body has to be used for the absent healing.

Q *Can you explain the process?*

YOU are like a television set. The spirit vibration comes to you and you transform it into the semi-physical healing ray to the patient. You are the transformer.

Q *In absent healing as well?*

YES.

Q *Then how does it get to the patient?*

BECAUSE the patient has made a request to you. Thought has created the vibration to you. There is the link, and through you it goes back on the same wavelength.

Absent healing

Q *How about if the patient doesn't know that absent healing has been asked on his behalf?*

SOMEONE must know otherwise you would not be giving absent healing.

Q *Well, you might know that the patient is not very well and you decide to give absent healing.*

THEN you have got the link there.

Q *But you haven't got the thought coming in.*

YES you have, you have created it. You must remember that thought is real on our plane of being. If I look at you, I don't see a physical body. I might if I could open the medium's eyes. It is your thought that is real to us, your body that is shadowy. The moment you send out any thought, that is a reality, that creates a vibration, a wavelength, and this is used in all the absent healing.

Q *Once a contact has been made for absent healing, is it necessary for it to be made again?*

NOT once the link is made. Every link with our world is a magnetic one. Once made it cannot be broken.

Q 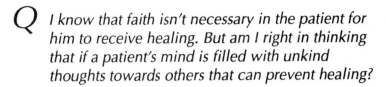 *I know that faith isn't necessary in the patient for him to receive healing. But am I right in thinking that if a patient's mind is filled with unkind thoughts towards others that can prevent healing?*

I DON'T object to faith, as long as it is founded on reason and is not blind faith. You who have this knowledge realise that what you have received is only an infinitesimal fraction of the totality of truth. It is not possible whilst you are encased in mortal bodies to receive all knowledge. You will not get it even when you come here. So you must have faith founded on what has been revealed to you. Now a reasoned faith, founded on knowledge, is admirable. I have no quarrel with that, because it creates the right atmosphere of optimism in which results can be obtained. The power of the spirit works best when you are bright and happy, cheerful and receptive, not when you are miserable, doubting, wavering and disturbing the atmosphere around you.

Q 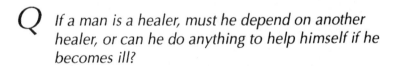 *If a man is a healer, must he depend on another healer, or can he do anything to help himself if he becomes ill?*

YOU need not depend on another healer, but you have to learn how to attune yourself to the power so that it can produce the result on you direct. Just as you do not have to go to church to pray to the Great Spirit, so you do not have to go to a healer to get healing, if you can enable the power of the spirit to come direct to you. You must open your heart, your mind, your soul.

Q 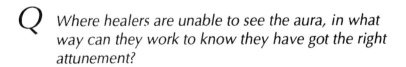 *Where healers are unable to see the aura, in what way can they work to know they have got the right attunement?*

IT does not matter whether the healer can see the aura. It does not matter whether the healer is able to diagnose. The object of the healer is to heal.

He should not concern himself with these other matters. He has to make himself accessible. He has to be as perfect an instrument as he can. He has to outlaw from his nature all the weaknesses that prevent him from being the perfect instrument. And the more he does that, the greater will be the power that flows through him. It is the life you live that qualifies the attunement you can have.

Q *Many healers are fortunate is being able to improve their gift by attending circles of instruction. What advice would you give to those who have no facilities for such development? Furthermore, do you consider that mediumship is essential to good healership?*

TO answer the second half, a clear emphatic 'No'. The gift of the spirit is the gift of the spirit. You are born with it and it is your responsibility to develop it, just as the child born with the gift of playing the piano has to develop it by practice and training. How to develop this gift? It is not the answer to sit in circles. That may help. It is developed by your motives. It is developed by the way you live your life. It is developed by the attempt to reach the highest standard of purity and perfection that is possible. It is helped by increasing your desire to heal as much as you possibly can.

The only way to develop self is to forget self. The more you think of others, the better self you will become. There is no book that will tell you how to become a better healer. What you have to do is to desire to serve, and order your life in this fashion: 'The Great Spirit has endowed me with a gift of healing. May I be worthy of it'. If you live your life according to that principle, the gift will automatically increase in its strength and stature.

Passing over after healing

 A person gets healing and improves, but later passes to your world. Why is this?

WHY is passing to our world a tragedy? In our world, when people are born into yours, we cry. When they come to our world, we rejoice. Why is it a tragedy to leave your earth?

Health of healers

 Would it not be best for all healers to be in perfect health themselves before they begin to heal others?

THOSE who heal by the power of the spirit are like other kinds of mediums – instruments. That is, they transmit something which they receive: they are channels, they turn it outward, not inward. The fact that they themselves may be suffering from some bodily affliction does not necessarily restrict their ability to heal others. One is a psychic quality, the other is a physical defect.

Disease

YOU get disease when the natural unity between man's triple nature of body, mind and spirit are out of harmony. Health is wholeness.

Healing of body, mind and spirit

WHAT is important is to touch souls. Then the power of the spirit can quicken the flicker of divinity into the beauteous, lambent flame, so that the majesty of latent divinity shines through, enabling their bodies to become well, their minds to learn the lessons and their spiritual natures to unfold further as a result.

Healing of body without touching soul

IF the soul is not touched, though the healing has touched the physical body, that is very sad. It means the sufferer has been given the opportunity of obtaining awareness and unfortunately has failed to take it. A healer must do the best he can, and allow the fullest amount of spirit power to pour through and work its divine will wherever it possibly can.

Not all souls can be receptive because that is not possible. A healer cannot cure everybody who comes to him. If you can obtain results with the hopeless cases, then that should be the clearest evidence to any with the ability to think and reason that a power vastly superior to matter has been at work.

Sickness

 Doctors say that some of the major sicknesses are due to pressure and business worries. In such cases how much does disharmony contribute?

YOU are saying the same thing as I said in different words. You are calling it a business worry, but that is a disharmony. If your mind, body and spirit are in the right relationship, you do not have worries of business or anything else. The soul that worries is out of harmony already. Anyone who has knowledge of spiritual realities should not worry. Worry and fear are the negative forces. They do not belong to the enlightened soul. You call it a business worry, I call it disharmony. There is nothing to worry about once you know you are an eternal being and nothing in the physical world can touch your soul.

Time spent on healing individuals

Q *Some healers only take a few minutes in their work on patients. Others take longer in varying degrees and the patient seems to get no better. Can you explain this please?*

BY their fruits ye shall know them! It is the results that matter. The healer should so live his life that he attains the greatest pitch of attunement. Then the results will come. You put your own house in order first. We will do the rest. No call for help is ever refused. No power is ever withheld. We always strive to serve. We refuse none. We welcome all. The power of the spirit is there for all to receive its beneficence. All we want are willing instruments to help its divine flow.

Healing – variable results

Q *A baby has two deformed legs. One responds and the other does not; why is that?*

BECAUSE the healing cannot produce results in both cases. The healing is never equal, it is always conditioned. It is characterised. It is very difficult because I want to keep this on the simplest possible plane. There are other qualifications, because there are laws within laws within laws that involve other and more profound issues. Healing is not as simple as it appears. It is not a question of just healing a physical ailment. It is soul qualities that have to be measured. What is the effect on the soul? What is the purpose? Why does the patient go to the healer? Has that patient reached the stage of spiritual evolution when his spirit can be awakened? There are matters you cannot measure with your material yardstick, but they are all involved in healing because you are handling the life force itself for the time being. You are partaking in the process of infinite creation. That is why I stress your great responsibility.

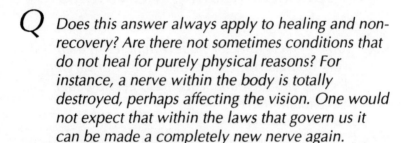

Q Does this answer always apply to healing and non-recovery? Are there not sometimes conditions that do not heal for purely physical reasons? For instance, a nerve within the body is totally destroyed, perhaps affecting the vision. One would not expect that within the laws that govern us it can be made a completely new nerve again.

WE are not talking about miracles.

Q Yes, but I thought you were generalising on the reason for non-recovery.

I AM saying that where the illness is capable of being healed, and the results are not obtained, that patient has not earned the spiritual right to be healed.

Mental sickness and help

Q We have every sympathy for the mentally sick yet we feel so helpless.

YOU can help the mentally sick. If you allow yourself to be used, that is all that is asked of you. Let the power flow through you. Those who cannot help by contact, send them absent healing. Spirit healing is here to stay. It will not be dislodged. You can contribute your quota, a very important quota it is too. Always remember you are a divine channel helping the Great Spirit in the infinite plan of evolution. It is a wonderful work you have to do, but it is as great responsibility.

Psychic surgery

Q *The success of an instantaneous healing depends on the patient's spiritual development, karma and other attributes. What happens in that respect in the case of a surgical 'operation' as performed by spiritual healers in Brazil and the Philippines?*

ALL this is regulated by cause and effect which is the natural law in operation. Whenever the soul of the individual is ready, then that person is influenced so that he or she is brought into the region where the healer is to operate. If the soul is ready, then the operation is a success. But, whatever occurs, even if a growth has been removed and the body is now free, it does not automatically follow that the patient will spiritually come into his own. It only means that he has spiritually arrived at the stage where he is ready, and this is his great chance for the spark now ignited to be fanned into a flame. So there are two factors in operation. The patient is spiritually ready, and that means he has been brought to the healer who can achieve the result. The patient now has the opportunity of spiritually coming into his own and living in the light of a spiritual awareness. If this does not happen then there has been a physical success but a spiritual failure.

Q *Is that kind of spiritual surgical healing a good way to heal?*

BY their fruits ye shall know them. The wind is tempered to the shorn lamb. All the outbreaks of spirit power are conditioned to the place and the time when they occur. The whole of the operation of mediumship and the outpouring of the power of the spirit are part of a planned, concerted effort. It is done primarily to meet the physical, mental and spiritual needs of the people to whom this applies. It is a question of temperament, education, environment, understanding, so that always the phenomena must take the form that will be most appropriate to those for whom they are intended.

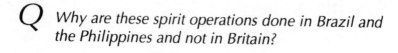

Q *Why are these spirit operations done in Brazil and the Philippines and not in Britain?*

THE spiritual climate is different; the mental climate is different. The needs are for more spectacularly striking results where minds are not yet conditioned to the more subtle influences of the spirit. It is somewhat similar to the conditions prevalent in your world just over one hundred years ago when it was necessary to demonstrate that kind of physical mediumship which would make the spiritual understandable in earthly terms. It is not necessary to do this now in Britain. But it still obtains in those countries where the standards of education, culture and appreciation are vastly different from those prevailing in this land. It must be suited to the people who dwell there.

Q *But there are a great number of people in this country who would very much like to see this type of operation and are unable to do so. Is climate an important factor?*

IT is partly climate because the atmosphere is more conducive. But it is also spiritual conditioning because it is not primarily suited for the people dwelling in your land. It is not a question of what people *want* to see but what is spiritually best for them. Too many prefer to have the highest spiritual elements reduced to the lowest physical level. This is not the way for advancement or progress.

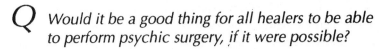

Q *Would it be a good thing for all healers to be able to perform psychic surgery, if it were possible?*

NO, there is not one road for all the instruments of the spirit. It is not uniformity that is desired but versatility and variety. Spirit is infinite and therefore has an infinite number of possible manifestations. It is all conditioned by the receptivity of the instrument. For that reason it is affected by the medium's temperament, upbringing, education, heredity, environment and even past incarnations. All these affect and qualify the kind, amount and type of spirit power that can function through any instrument. It is not for all to follow the same path. You will find the answer in the Bible where it says "Now there are diversities of gifts, but the same spirit!"

Q *The purer the instrument the more healing power can flow through him or her. Does this also apply in psychic surgery?*

THE question is not correctly stated. It is not true that the purer the instrument the more power can flow through him. Power can flow through an instrument that is not so pure. The quality of the power is affected by the purity of the instrument. Spirit power is infinite, like the Creator, the Great Spirit. Because it is infinite it has an infinite number of gradations, variations, combinations. The individual tunes into that stage for which he is spiritually ready. He cannot get any higher spiritually because he could not receive it and naturally he would not want to go lower. No, it is the quality of the power that is affected by the development, the attainment, the stage that the instrument has reached, not the quantity.

Heart transplants

AS a principle I am opposed to transplants. I don't question the sincerity of those who offer bodily parts to be used in the service of others.

The Great Spirit has endowed every human with a physical body to express the spirit that is responsible for its life. This is an intimate relationship between the body and the spirit. If it were necessary for transplants then you would not have the failures when hearts and kidneys are transplanted into other bodies.

 What are the spiritual aspects of heart transplant surgery?

MOTIVE is always the important consideration. Undoubtedly in some cases the motive is to sustain earthly life. It can be that experimentation encourages an enthusiasm for more experimentation which in the end is not concerned with the prolongation of earthly life. Also, it must be said that subjecting helpless animals to cruelty in order to learn from them is not an act that can be considered to have any spiritual value. Not through cruelty will man find health. Not through exploitation will he learn the secrets of nature that have so far eluded him.

I am not in favour of the transfer of any bodily organ from one to another. Indeed, I am not in favour of the transfusion of blood. I do not think, from my point of view, and I speak only for myself, that the sustaining of the physical body must be the be-all of every endeavour. I maintain that man should be instructed how to live aright, spiritually, mentally and physically. If he thinks right, then he behave right and his body will be right.

The solution is not the transfer of bodily parts. The solution is for every man to order himself to live as the Great Spirit intended. Man must have compassion for other men and for all the creatures with whom he shares his planet. They were not placed here by the Great Spirit to be used as experiments, to prolong the physical life of man.

 Is it right to say at this stage that the heart transplant must be doomed to failure?

IT is conceivable that there may be some successful experiments. What I am concerned with is that the experiments are taking the wrong spiritual turning. This is not the direction in which those who should be dedicated to man's well-being should be working. They will not bring health. Health is harmony. These are merely attempts at a temporary patching up of bodies.

You must understand the simple essence. You are created body, mind and spirit. These are indivisible; they are not exchangeable parts. You are a whole individual. To achieve health you must have wholeness, harmony, rhythm, concert, between your tripartite being. This is the only way you can get health, not through drugs, not through medicines. These are temporary reliefs. Your world is full of ignorance. Death is the dread monster to be evaded. Death is feared, but death is part of the natural law. Physical immortality is not the object of earthly existence. The earth is the training ground, the school to learn your lessons for the greater life that must inevitably be yours.

Life support machines

WHEN the time comes for the spirit to leave the body there is no machine in your world that can make it stay. It is not in the power of anyone in your world to compel the spirit to stay once the cord has been cut because then physical death has occurred.

Organ removal

I know about transplants, and am aware that the motive is often a very good one. But I must say that I am opposed to transplanting any part of the human body to other people.

Prolonging physical life medically

NO medical man can keep a man alive when it is time for that individual to die.

As I understand it, your doctors are uncertain when death comes. There are controversies as to the exact moment of death. Death is final when the silver cord is severed and the spirit body leaves the physical one. That is the only time that death occurs. When that severance has taken place, no medical man can make that body live again.

LIFE AFTER DEATH

Life After Death

Children

Q *In the next world, we know that children grow up to become adults; but what about those guides who remain children for many years on earth, and also children who have been dead for 18-20 years who still return as children?*

YOUR hard bitter world condemns those who go on being children, and claims all the time that it loves the innocence of the child. Yet it objects to them when they choose to persist in that form of evolution solely to help. The child is not beset by the many problems that perplex adults and therefore is the best channel for communication.

In the case of the ordinary child who comes back after many years still as a child, this is done for recognition.

Links after passing

Q *Do the loved ones who have gone into the spirit world always know what the people left on earth are thinking?*

IF they are loved ones, that is, if there is love between them. I must try to be a little more explicit. The people who dwell in my world are not always eavesdropping, but those who are bound by ties of love are still together, despite the incident of death. What your world does not understand is that those who are called dead are still there. It is not as if they are in another universe; it is all part of the same universe. All life is one life, but with millions of gradations. The unfortunate part is that the awareness that they are present is not realised by the people of your earth, but the ones who have died, as you call it, are close, just as close, and in many cases closer than they have ever been before. Now, having transferred their expression of life from a material phase to a spiritual one, all the faculties of the spirit are the reality, and the attributes of the body are shadowy, so that to those who love you, your thoughts are more real than your words. But if there is no love, then there is no tie, there is no association, for on the spiritual plane love is the guiding principle.

Appreciation of beauty

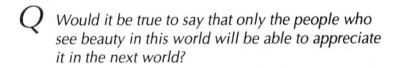

Q *Would it be true to say that only the people who see beauty in this world will be able to appreciate it in the next world?*

NO, it would be very unfair, for millions are unable to appreciate any beauty because they lack the educational facilities that enable them to have a true standard of appreciation. Our world is a world not only of retribution, but also of compensation, where all that you lacked in your earthly life is given to you so that a true balance may be struck.

Communication in the after-life

WHEN you come to our world you do not have physical bodies. You have their replicas, but you do not have speech. Except in the comparatively lower realms you realise there is a superior method of communication, mind to mind direct, without the necessity of using language which is a very clumsy substitute for thought. Thought is superior to language.

Divine justice

Q *How does an avowed materialist fare when he passes over?*

YOUR world for too long has been deluded with the idea that the ones who call themselves religious possess a spiritual advantage over their fellows. That is not axiomatic. You are not the spiritual superior of your fellows because you believe in certain theological doctrines. The only test which is applied is the test of daily life. Your spiritual nature is exactly what you made it to be, and there are many materialists and atheists and rationalists and agnostics who are the spiritual superiors of thousands who think that they are amongst the elect because they have bowed the knee in homage to the Great Spirit and accept certain doctrines. The test is not what you believe, but what you have done, otherwise there would be a complete mockery of divine justice.

You cannot limit divine justice. Being divine it will operate, just like nature, irrespective of what you wish, think or desire. You cannot make comparisons between divine and human justice. Human justice is fallible, makes mistakes, the innocent is sometimes guilty and the guilty is sometimes innocent. Being human you must err, because you cannot be infallible.

Death

Grieving

BUT do please try to understand this, death is not tragedy to those who die; it is only a tragedy to those who are left behind. To go from darkness to light is not something over which you should grieve. If you grieve, you are in reality grieving over your loss and not for one who has in truth become enfranchised. He is better off. He will no longer suffer all the ills of the human body. He will not be subjected to the ravages of wasting diseases. He will unfold all the gifts with which he has been endowed, and will express them free from any thwartings and will be able to give a larger service to those who require it.

Do not mourn because the caterpillar has become a beauteous butter-fly. Do not weep because the cage has been opened and the bird has been set free. Rejoice and know that the enfranchised soul has found liberty and that, if you would but unfold the powers that the Great Spirit has given you, you could share some of the new beauty and joy which is theirs. You could understand the plan of death and realise that death is but a stepping stone, a door through which you enter into the larger freedom of the realms of the spirit.

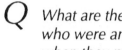 *What are the feelings of people like H.G. Wells, who were anti-Spiritualist and lifelong rationalists, when they pass on and find themselves in a spirit world in which they do not believe?*

IT is a complete overthrow of a lifetime of philosophy and they cannot understand it. They think there must be something wrong with the universe because it does not agree with their conceptions, which they had proved most logically and most scientifically. And so the adjustments have to be made and there are long arguments and discussions.

 When a person dies, what likeness do they retain? Could a husband be unrecognisable to a wife who passed on twenty or thirty years after? Could he progress so much that he was out of the orbit of his wife?

YOU do not change your identity. You do not change your individuality; you do not change your consciousness. You grow in spiritual grace and stature, but you are the same individual that you were before – with your perceptions heightened, your faculties deepened. But, except for the disappearance of blemishes, defects and injuries, you are recognisable as you were on earth. You do not change your form, for all that is spiritual still requires a mode of manifestation, a body, a vehicle, an instrument through which the spirit must register itself. And that has always existed, that finer, more rarefied, more delicate body, while you were on earth.

 Does the way you die have any effect when you reach the spirit world; if you die just naturally, is it easier to get to the spirit world or not?

OH yes, it makes a very big difference. If everyone in your world had knowledge and lived natural lives then the process of what we call dying would be simple and free from any pain. Also, it would be unnecessary to have any adjustment to the body of the spirit after the physical body had died. But unfortunately that does not take place.

The vast majority of those who leave your world for ours are profoundly ignorant of their destiny, of their own constitution and of the nature of spiritual realities. In addition, there are far, far too many who come to us before their time is ripe, and as I so often say, they are like the fruit which crops from the tree before it is ready – as you know then the fruit is not very good. When fruit is ripe it naturally drops, and when your spirit is ripe, the physical body should drop naturally away from you. And so we have today sour and green fruit coming to us. Because of that they have to be tended, watched over, cared for, nursed, until the adjustments are made. If all had knowledge, then the work of those who like myself are striving to help would be far easier.

Certainly the way you die makes a tremendous difference. Dying is the sloughing off of the physical body as the spiritual body gradually emerges. It is never a painful process. There may be some physical reactions when there is illness or disease. If the transition is not a simple one, then the equivalent of your doctors stand by. They help those who love this individual to accomplish his or her birth into our world until the cord connecting spirit and matter severs itself and separation is assured for all time.

The question of awakening is the next to be considered. This depends on the degree of awareness that the newcomer possesses. If completely ignorant of the fact that life continues after earthly death, or if so indoctrinated with false ideas that understanding will take a long time, then there is a process of rest and equivalent to sleep.

That continues until it is self-determined that the time for realisation has come. This can be short or long, as measured by your duration of time. It depends upon the individual. Those with knowledge have no such problems. They step out of the world of matter into the world of spirit and the adjustment is speedy. When awakening comes it is a moment of supreme joy because it brings recognition of all loved ones who have been waiting for it to occur.

There is nothing to fear in death. Death is the great liberator; death brings freedom. You rejoice when babies come into your world. There are many who cry in our world when babies are about to be born into your world. Similarly, there is weeping when people die in your world, but there is rejoicing in ours. Death means that the life has served its purpose, or should have done, and the individual is ready to enjoy all the tremendous richness and beauty that the spirit life has to offer.

Believing

 You said so many people arrive in the spirit world with false teaching. In St. John's Gospel it says believing is the important part.

NO. Everyone will live after what you call death, not because of believing in a creed, a doctrine or a dogma, but because it is an unalterable natural law. It has nothing to do with religion. It is a law equal to the law of cause and effect.

Other Side: where is it?

IT is the invisible and the inaudible side of the world in which you live. You are as much now in the world of spirit as you ever will be. You will not go there when you pass from your world, you are in the spirit world now. You cannot register it unless you have developed the gifts of the spirit so that you can tune in to all its vibrations and frequencies, or whatever word you care to use. It is not another world. It is an integral part of the universe of which earth is but one aspect.

Q *Many people when they pass on have no knowledge of the after-life. They are in a kind of daze and do not know that they have passed on. Does this apply to children?*

IT depends on the child's knowledge. If it has not been too tainted with the ignorance and superstition of your world, then its natural understanding based on its natural psychic powers, will enable a natural appreciation to occur.

Q *How long does it take before a spirit comes back to this world after death takes place?*

IT depends on the conditions. There are some who come into our world who, although they have been here for centuries, have not yet awakened to the realisation of what has taken place. And there are some who come here with knowledge, who know the ropes, and to them, if they can find the right medium, they can manifest within a few moments of passing. There is no simple answer.

Facets of the soul

 You say the soul is divided into many parts. Only one part can come to earth. Are the others progressing in other spheres?

WE have to use words which are very poor symbols for that which is beyond all your language. Words are physical. The soul is non-physical. How do we interpret the non-physical in physical language? This is a great problem of what you call semantics. To me the soul is that part of the divinity within each one of you, what you call God, and I the Great Spirit. There are no means of measuring souls in terms that you can understand. The soul is the life force, the dynamic, the vitality, the real essence, the divinity.

You think of souls in terms of personalities and individuals. If I ask, "Who are you?" I don't know how you would answer. Giving me your name does not tell me who you are. That is only the name by which you are called. Who are you, the individual, the judge, the thinker, the one who expresses love and is capable of manifesting all the emotions that form the spectrum of human experience in your world? That is the soul.

You live on earth because the soul provides animation for the physical body. When the soul withdraws, the physical body, having no animation, dies. That soul has not a name, such as you are called by in your world. Because it is divine it is infinite. And being infinite it is capable of an infinite number of manifestations. The soul has many aspects. I use the simile of a diamond with many facets. Those facets can incarnate into your world at differing times to gain experience, to help the other facets in the diamond's evolution towards perfection.

Where you have affinities, which is rare, it is because they are two facets of the same diamond incarnating at the same time on earth. That is why there is complete harmony between them. They are parts of the one whole. This brings us to the subject of reincarnation. Here you have facets of the diamond incarnating into your world to add knowledge, development and experience that will help the diamond in its evolution.

Facets of life

Q *You mention a facet of a large diamond, that I could be one of a group soul of people. It does not seem logical, if we have eternity, that it would be necessary for me to have experience for a number of other souls.*

ACTION and reaction occur throughout the whole universe. Man in faraway places can produce a tremendous impact on your existence in the way of contributing to the sum total of knowledge everywhere. You cannot live in physical, mental and spiritual isolation. Call it group, call it a diamond, you are trying to use words to express what is beyond words. Who are "you", and when did "you" begin? Did your individuality commence from the moment of conception? "Before Abraham was, I am," said the Nazarene. What did he mean? Only that as spirit he had always existed; so have you and so have I. It may be that fragments incarnate at differing times. I have no quarrel with those who will not accept what I say. I always tell my friends to reject what their reason cannot accept. If we would win affection, and perhaps your love, it must be because reason tells you we say what is true. If we cannot win your affection with reason, then we must be failing in our purpose. We must build on the knowledge that we have, making sure that its base is secure. From that, let us explore the higher paths as we ascend, slowly, gradually.

You have much to make you rejoice. Problems you will always meet, difficulties you will always encounter. You are not perfect beings living in a perfect world. You are imperfect and your world is imperfect. But you have free will and a wonderful opportunity of helping to rid the world of its imperfections and yourself of your imperfections. This is your task. Whatever knowledge you have gained, the greater is the responsibility as to how you use it. A trust is reposed in you. You must not betray it. You must show by your own life that you are worthy, not only of the knowledge that you have received, but ready for the next knowledge to come to you as it will when you are ready to receive it.

Untouched souls

Q *What happens to the souls who are not touched here on earth?*

THIS is very difficult. It is akin to what happens to adults who face life without having had any education of any kind. They start with complete unawareness. They are the misfits in your world and in ours. It means they have not learned the lessons that should equip them for our life. They are unready, unprepared.

Q *How can you help them?*

SOME of them have to incarnate again in your world because we cannot do very much for a soul who has no awareness. It can take hundreds of years as you measure time to bring that awareness to them.

Q *Are they helped by their spirit friends?*

AS much as they can be helped. But until awareness comes there is darkness. Without awareness light cannot penetrate.

Materialism and untouched souls

YOU should feel sorry for them because they have wasted their earthly lives. They have not fulfilled themselves. They are like children who have gone to school for the requisite time, learnt none of its lessons and thus are not equipped for the adult life that follows when the school period is over. Earth is an essential preparation for the existence that inevitably follows when death comes. Every happening is part of the price to be paid for evolution. Earthly life cannot be a monotone. It must have its light and shade, its sunshine and storm.

Time needed for a state of peace

IT depends on whether the individual has any knowledge of spiritual matters. If there is ignorance, there can be temporary harm to the soul. Even when the cord connecting the physical and spiritual bodies is cut, there is still a certain amount of interplay due to long association of the two forms of being.

Generally it is considered advisable, where there is complete ignorance of spiritual truths, for an interval of three days to elapse before there is either burial or cremation.

Group soul

 Are group souls family groups, people in the same state of spiritual development, those with the same interests, or what else?

IF the questioner uses the word "family" in its literal sense, as you understand it, being confined to people who have blood ties or relationships due to marriage, then this does not apply to group souls. Earthly ties, which are purely material, do not necessarily continue when the body has served its purpose.

In spiritual relationships, you have in the supreme case affinities or in the lesser instances kinship. Physical relationships are conditions not based on eternal principles, the only ones that will endure. Group souls, when referring to their human aspects, are composed of individuals who have a spiritual kinship. Automatically they are drawn to one another because they are facets of the same diamond. It can be, and it does happen, that for purposes of work to be done fragments of the diamond incarnate into your world to have the kind of experience which will help the larger self.

Guidance

 Does guidance come from a general or particular source, and can prayer and meditation lead one to discern this?

SHALL I repeat words that are very familiar? When the pupil is ready the master appears. Is that not the answer? Do not bother about it. All guidance streams from the Great Spirit. Ambassadors from the hierarchy and other enlightened beings, who are kindred souls as far as you are concerned, attach themselves to you sometimes before you are born into your world.

Sometimes they make themselves known to you before you incarnate into your world, sometimes you agree with them that you will volunteer to perform certain tasks. It does not matter what names you call them. They are there. They do not leave you. Their task, as it says in your Bible, "He shall give his angels charge concerning thee."

Reincarnation

 Is it possible for one's consciousness to function in separate portions?

THERE is a consciousness which is you, of which you in the world of matter are expressing but a tiny portion, and there are portions of that same consciousness which are expressing themselves in other spheres of expression.

Q Independently?

NO, not independently. You and the other expressions are all reflections of one inner spiritual reality. They are parts of a whole and the fragments are expressing themselves as parts of the whole, but through different vehicles of expression, which sometimes coalesce. They are not ignorant of each other within themselves, but only when they first begin to express themselves, until they find a common meeting-place and fit together into the whole once again.

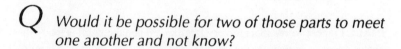

Q Would it be possible for two of those parts to meet one another and not know?

TRY to picture the greater consciousness as a circle, and then realise that there are segments of that circle which are revolving round its centre. Sometimes those segments meet and when they meet there is a recognition of their common oneness. When they finally cease to revolve, the different segments occupy their allotted places and the circle is united and complete.

Q Is it possible for two parts of the same spirit to communicate with each other?

IF it is necessary.

Q Are sometimes two parts of the same spirit incarnated on earth at the same time?

NO, for that would be contrary to the whole purpose. The purpose of the individual is to find experience on all planes of expression and only to return to the same plane when there is something to be achieved by the return.

Q *Would it be true to say that each reflection of the spirit has to work out its own progress, and the common benefit from the lessons learned by other reflections of the same spirit?*

YES, they are all parts of the one soul which express themselves in different forms. You become increasingly conscious of more and more of yourself.

Q *And there is a point in evolution at which all those different parts are joined?*

YES, in infinity.

Q *Would it be true to say that each of these sections incarnate only once and that, while reincarnation would be true when considering the complete soul, it would be untrue of each section?*

IT depends on what has to be fulfilled. Only when some special mission has to be performed would the same portion of consciousness incarnate more than once.

Q *What do you mean by different parts of the same consciousness?*

IT is hard to answer you because you do not understand what living really means. Life to you has expressed itself particularly in its lowest forms. You cannot visualize real life, living intensely in a consciousness that is superior to anything which you conceive.

The highest experience of the mystic, the greatest inspiration of the artist, the rapture of the poet – even these are but faint shadows of the reality which we call life in spirit realms. When you cannot appreciate that, because your expression is limited to a world of matter that vibrates slowly, how can I explain to you what consciousness is and how it is able to register itself?

Do you see my difficulty? If you had a measure of comparison it would be easier, but you can only compare light with darkness, sunshine with shadow. You cannot compare the colours of the rainbow with colours that are beyond your means of understanding and appreciation.

Q Are they different virtues or facets of characters that are split?

NO, not at all. It is not another facet of the individuality at all. When you ask these questions it is like trying to explain to one who has been blind from birth what the colour of the sky looks like when the sun is shining. You have no standard of comparison.

Q Does not your explanation of "split" consciousness express the same truth as F.W.H. Myers's declaration regarding "group" souls?

IT is really the same thing, except that it is not a grouping of different souls, but a union of the different portions of consciousness returning to complete the whole.

Q It seems that when the different parts of consciousness are reunited each would lose its own individuality.

DOES the stream lose itself when it flows into the mighty ocean, or is the ocean many streams? Does the note of the violin lose itself when it merges into the harmony created by the whole orchestra?

Q *Why does not the spirit world give us proof of reincarnation?*

WHAT could be evidence of reincarnation that you could not explain by spirit control? You will only accept it when your consciousness is ready, when it becomes clear to you that it is the law. That is why there are many in my world who say it does not happen. They say it does not happen because they have not yet reached the stage of consciousness when they know it does happen. Can a mystic explain his mysticism to a man of business? Can an artist explain to those not endowed with his sensitiveness what his inspiration is? He cannot. They are on different mental planes.

Q *Does the soul know when it is about to reincarnate?*

THE soul knows, but cannot express itself through the mind. The soul, which is the Great Spirit, expresses itself through all eternity, gradually, step by step, and at any stage there is a vast portion still not expressed.

Q *Is it, then, unconsciously done when a soul reincarnates?*

IT depends on the state of evolution of that soul. There are many souls who know they have incarnated before. There are others who do not. Their souls may know, their consciousness may know, but it may not be known by the mind. You are touching the greatest mysteries of life, and I find it very hard to discover words in your English language to express the things of the spirit.

Q *If life is continual change and evolution, and reincarnation is a fact, how can we be sure of meeting our loved ones when we pass over, and of enjoying the life of bliss with them promised to us?*

LOVE will always know its own, for love is the greatest force in the universe. Love will always attract its beloved and love will always meet its love, for nothing can prevent the union of those who love.

Q *But with reincarnation there will be continual separation. Does that fit in with the idea of eternal bliss?*

YOUR idea of eternal bliss does not fit in with my idea of eternal bliss. The universe and the laws in it are as the Great Spirit made them, not as His children make them. The wise man changes his mind as he faces new facts, because he knows that he cannot alter the facts to please his fancy.

Q *If it is true that we have been through countless lives before this one, why is it that we are not more progressed and ideal than we are?*

YOU can be in the world of matter and be a saint; you can be in the world of matter and be the lowest of the low. It does not depend on the earthly plane. It depends on the evolution of the soul.

Q *Have we still an infinite number of suffering and struggling lives to go through in the future, as in the past?*

YES, infinite. Struggle, suffering, through the crucible of pain does the Great Spirit express itself... Suffering tries the Great Spirit. Suffering enables the Great Spirit within to emerge purified, strengthened, refined, even as the gold emerges from the ore by crushing, by refining. Until it has been through these processes, it is not revealed as gold.

Q *If that is so, what is the use of the ideas of a heaven after death?*

THAT which you consider heaven today you will not consider heaven tomorrow, for happiness consists in striving, always striving, for the higher and the higher beyond that.

Q *If a soul is reincarnated, does it come back to the same nationality as it functioned in the last incarnation – Indian to Indian and British to British, for example?*

NOT necessarily. It will choose that country and that race which is necessary for its new unfoldment.

Q *Does the same thing apply in matters of sex?*

YES. It does not necessarily come back to the same sex that it had before.

Q *Can it be true that we are punished for our sins in another life on earth, as well as having to atone before we can progress in the spirit world? Would God punish us twice for the same sin?*

IT is not always a question of punishment, but of evolution, of a task to be learned, of another link to be forged in the chain of the soul's education and upliftment. Reincarnation does not always mean that you are to be punished. It often means that there are gaps to be filled. Sometimes they are chastening ones, sometimes they are lessons which have not been learned. It does not always mean punishment. You cannot be punished twice. When you have an understanding of the Law you will marvel at its perfection, for it cannot be unevenly weighted on one side. The Law is perfect because the Great Spirit is perfect.

 Can you tell of anyone on the Other Side who knows for a certainty that he or she has gone through one or more periods of reincarnation in this world?

YES. When the soul has evolved to the stage where it is necessary for it to know, it knows. It cannot see the light until its eyes can stand the light. I will not give names for they would not be evidence. I have said before that all which is true of reincarnation can be "explained" by control.

I speak of the laws of the Great Spirit as far as my own understanding reaches. I only speak the truth as I know it. If there are some who do not agree, I do not mind. It does not matter if others do not accept it. When they have lived as long as I have, they may change their minds.

 There is a lot of controversy regarding reincarnation. Would it not be wiser to concern ourselves with survival?

IT is better to be in the light than in the dark. It is better to have knowledge than ignorance. It is better to know the laws than not to know the laws. It is better always to search for truth, diligently and patiently, rather than to sit still. It is always better to strive for progress. Survival is not the end. It is only the beginning, for when you understand that you are a part of the Great Spirit and because of that you pass through the avenue of death, unharmed and unchanged, that is not the end of all things. That is only the beginning.

EARTHLY LIFE

EARTHLY LIFE

Abortion – at what point is it wrong?

THE answer is from the very minute it is done it is wrong. Listen, you have no power to create life. You have power to transfer life. You have no right to destroy its expression. Abortion is akin to murder. From the moment of conception the spirit has incarnated into a woman's womb. When it is aborted it will continue to be a spiritual body, however immature, and grow and develop. You may have destroyed the means of physical expression, but you have not destroyed the spirit that was there. Abortion is interference with the embryonic spirit which is developing according to its natural growth. There are qualifications when the motive is right. That will always be taken into account.

I do not know of any evolved being in my world who favours abortion. But always there is the qualification that the motive must be taken into consideration. The act itself is condemned.

You do not create life. You should not therefore end the means by which it expresses itself. If those who practice abortion realised they were not merely getting rid of matter, but a living entity with whom one day they will be confronted, I think there would be fewer abortions. From the moment of conception, there is the beginning of an individual, who will never die and continue to grow in my world.

Accidental death

I AM not happy about the word "accident" because I know only of cause and effect in operation. Whatever you regard as accidental can be due only to the operation of the law of cause and effect.

Q *If a child dies as a result of an accident, was that intended by the Great Spirit?*

THE whole of life is controlled by law. The Great Spirit is responsible for law. But law works through human beings. You have intelligence and reasoning. If you choose to put your head under a train it is no use blaming the Great Spirit.

Air disasters

Q *Are they planned as karmic debt of victims and their relatives? If planned, why do people have premonitions of them, as these sometimes change the whole course of events?*

THIS is quite a question. I don't like the word "planned". It presupposes that there is a deliberate attempt to plan a tragedy in your world. Everything that happens is due to cause and effect. As to the victims – I must use your language – of these tragedies, do not forget that there is another side to the picture.

Death to people in your world is something to be feared. But death to us is something of the nature of rejoicing. There are many in our world who cry when babies are born into yours. We rejoice when death brings freedom to those who die.

It may be hard to understand, but destiny has its part in the great eternal scheme. This is a complex subject in which fate and free will play their parts. Both are true. There is a restricted free will within the destined fate. This is the simplest way that I can put it.

As to the premonitions, these occur because individuals momentarily remove themselves from their usual three dimensional and are able to experience, however fleetingly, time as it exists in its own sphere. What you must try to realise is that time is an eternal present. It is your earthly relationship to time that determines what you call past and future. If you escape the three dimensional barriers and get in touch with time as it really is, then you are aware of what is the future to you at the present time.

Now as to what use is made of this awareness is another matter. It can appeal purely on a super physical level or on a spiritual one. The purely psychic is not the same as the spiritual. You have what you call "extra sensory perception" which can have no relationship to your spiritual nature, but be merely an extension of your physical senses.

Age

DO not confuse physical age with spiritual maturity. It is not the number of years that matters, but the growth development and unfoldment of the soul that is temporarily manifested through the body.

It is not the plan of the Great Spirit to increase the number of physical years that your body should exist in your world.

What should happen is that when the spirit is ready the body will die, just as the apple drops from the tree when it is ripe. So forget the physical years. They do not matter.

The whole object and essence of earthly life is to enable the spirit to have the kind of exercise, education and experience that fit it to begin its life in our world.

If the spirit does not have the experience to equip it for our world, then it is like a child who has gone to school, has not learned the lessons, and is not ready for the adult life that follows.

Anaesthetic

Q *Where is the spirit, or that part which survives after death, when a person is under an anaesthetic?*

I DO not know. It might be anywhere. It depends on the evolution of the person as to how far it can go and where it goes.

Anguish

Q *Does anguish come from within or without?*

IT can be both. What you must appreciate is that earthly life provides a polarity which is not available in our world. In our world people of the same stage of evolution are in the same spiritual sphere or plane.

In your world you are mixing all the time with people of varying stages of evolution. You get opportunities for all the opposites to be encountered. Thus you can have light and dark, heat and cold. All this is the purpose of earthly life. It provides the means by which the soul comes into its own.

Armageddon

Q *Is there any truth in the prophecy of a rapidly approaching, final Armageddon?*

NO, there is no truth in the idea of an approaching Armageddon. What must be realised is that all the people who helped to compile the Bible were, in greater or lesser degree, psychic and, like all those endowed with the gifts of the spirit, their inspiration came to them in symbolic form. Now spiritual things must be spiritually discerned. You must not read symbolism as reality. The impress of our world on yours is in pictorial representation and it is for you to interpret that which is received. It is not true that there will be a final Armageddon in which the whole world of matter will be destroyed and then the Nazarene will come once more in the flesh to be acclaimed Lord of all the world. All life is part of evolution and there is no end to the physical world. It will improve, it will grow, it will evolve. And man improves and grows and evolves. In all life there is no beginning and no end.

 Is it of any use that Armistice Services should go on, year after year?

IT is better to remember those you call dead for two minutes than not to think of them at all. But I do not see what good can come when you celebrate the Armistice with a display of military might, with rifles and bayonets, with soldiers, with the firing of maroons and with all that comes with war. Could you not have an Armistice that was a spiritual service?

 Would it not be folly for Great Britain to refrain from arming in view of the undoubted fact that other great powers of Europe are armed to the teeth?

HAVE I not already said so many times that you think in terms of one country and one people while I think in terms of the Great Spirit and all his children? I tell you that you will not find peace by making machines of destruction. You find peace when there is a desire for peace and when all people live by the law of love and service. I do not think only of one country and one race of people. I think of all peoples as one, as part of the Great Spirit. They are all his children.

Until you apply his laws to your world of matter, you will have war and destruction, pestilence, havoc, chaos and bankruptcy all over again.

Astral travel

IT happens very simply that the real you leaves your body and is able to travel vast distances, sometimes into our world, and sometimes into the further reaches of your world. Actually every one of you travels astrally when you go to sleep.

Automatic writing

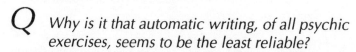 *Why is it that automatic writing, of all psychic exercises, seems to be the least reliable?*

IT all depends on the mediums. If they are not developed, they cannot distinguish between the thoughts that they pick up from your world and the thoughts which come to them from ours. That is a matter of development, for as the mediumship unfolds so it begins to reject the impressions of your world and becomes more susceptible to the influence of our world. You must not blame us because your instruments are not developed. We can only work with the material that you give us.

Birth

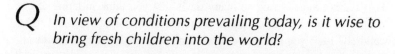 *In view of conditions prevailing today, is it wise to bring fresh children into the world?*

WE teach personal responsibility. Though the world is filled with chaos, anxiety and strife; though it is filled with bitterness, antagonism and hatred, a new world is fashioned out of the striving and miseries which are endured. Some there must be who are to become its standard bearers. The race must go on. The spirit must perfect itself through struggle, difficulty and labour. Humanity marches onward, not because it treads an easy path, but because it conquers all difficulty and emerges triumphant. Fear is always the worst enemy, it is born of man's ignorance.

Birth control

YOU have been given free will and a conscience to distinguish between that which is wrong and that which is right. It always depends on the motive. Say that once. Say it a hundred times. What is your motive? It is that which counts, nothing else.

Broadcast explanation

 If you were asked to broadcast on the truth of Spiritualism, what would you say?

LIFE cannot die. I tell you that you are immortal, deathless, that the ones for whom you have mourned, for whom the tears of sorrow have streamed down your cheeks, stand silently by your side – silent to you because you cannot hear them, but their voices have cried out in anguish for a long time in their striving to reach you. You are the dead, the dead who are unconscious of life as it really exists. You have closed your eyes to all the beauties of the Great Spirit's universe.

You have allowed yourself to register only the infinitesimal fraction of an earthly world. All around you the whole atmosphere teems with a multitudinous life. If you are wise you will open the windows of your souls, so that you can become aware of that mighty power of the spirit which will strengthen you and encourage you.

Brotherhood

WE preach the gospel of the spiritual brotherhood of all peoples, with the Great White Spirit as the common father. What stands in the way is the earthly conception, the churches built on error, the usurping of privilege, the pride and the power of tyrants, petty tyrants who hold the whip hand.

As our teaching grows in your world, it will mean the end of separateness between peoples. It will mean the end of national barriers. It will mean the end of race distinctions, class distinctions, colour distinctions and all the distinctions between churches and chapels, temples, mosques and synagogues, for gradually all will learn that they have a part of the Great Spirit's truth and that the part enshrined in the heart of every other religion in no way contradicts that portion that is precious to them.

Capital punishment

I HAVE never hesitated to say what I regard is spirit teaching: that one murder does not justify another. The people of your world must distinguish between justice and revenge. To send any soul unprepared into our world may justify the lowest passions of humans in your world, but it accomplishes nothing. Justice should be done. By your world performing murder it has not increased by one iota its spiritual upward evolution. Instead it has descended and indulged in "an eye for an eye and a tooth for a tooth". When passion usurps reason what follows cannot be right.

We must adhere to principles which we know are true because they are founded on the indisputable fact that life continues after physical death. You create more and more troubles by sending into our world people who are unprepared for it. In some cases the execution is performed on the wrong individual and justice is not done.

Life is sacred and is not yours to give or take away. Life is your responsibility. Life is not created by matter. Matter is created and sustained by life. Life is of the spirit, life emanates from the Great Spirit, life is divine. When you deal with life and its expressions you should always adopt the highest standards of mercy, compassion and sympathy. Make sure that your motive is right in whatever you do.

You will not solve your problems that way at all. Love is the fulfilling of the law. Whatever you do must be an attempt to help, not to exact revenge.

Another murder does not excuse the first one. Killing by the state does not solve any situation. If you meet force by force you are not encouraging the power of goodness, compassion and kindness to be exercised.

All punishment must be remedial and redemptive. The object should always be to enable the soul to come into its own. To send into our world souls that are unready merely increases problems. It does not lessen them in your world or in ours. Besides, you can make mistakes.

Children

Q *Is it fitting for children to be born into this pitiful world?*

AS far as I see it, the answer is to be found in human free will. I do not think that the word "pitiful" is a fair description of your world, though such a blackness covers many parts of it. The earth has its part to play in a universe of ordered creation. The earth is one of the steps in the ladder of life. It is one of the spheres of being through which every individual has to pass as part of the equipment, the training for the spirit. If the earth were not necessary, then the earth would not exist. The fact that it does exist is evidence of the part it plays in the divine, evolutionary scheme.

Communication in the spirit world . . .

UNTIL people learn to commune without speech, speech is used.

. . . and the Earth and higher planes

Q *When spirits who have left the astral plane communicate with the earth, do they have to come down to the astral plane to do so?*

OH, no. They can always find others through whom their message can be transmitted. They can always use instruments, but they would have to be evolved not only beyond the astral but much more than that. It must not be supposed that only those in the astral, which is the next stage beyond the physical, can communicate with your world of matter, for that is not so. For many states or spheres beyond that it is possible to have direct communication, always depending on your finding an instrument in the world of matter capable of receiving your vibrations.

Communicating spirits

Q Does the communicating spirit know whether he has registered on our consciousness in sleep state?

NO, not always. We do not always know at seances, at the time, how much is transmitted. It is often the same when impressing people.

Compensation and retribution

Q If a person has been good, will he suffer in any way for not believing the truth of survival, even if he has been told of it?

GOOD, bad – I do not know what these words mean. It will depend only on the life he has led, the service he has rendered, the opportunities he has taken to unfold the Great Spirit that is within him. That is all that counts. It is better to have knowledge than ignorance, but the only test is the way you have lived your life from day to day.

Conception

Q *At what point after conception does a spirit enter the body of a baby?*

I KNOW that many will not agree with me, but I say that from the moment the two seeds have become one and there is provided in that very miniature form a vehicle through which a spirit can function, from that moment the spirit starts its earthly career.

Conduct

Q *How should a Spiritualist conduct himself or herself in these times?*

THOSE with knowledge should never allow fear to find a lodgement within them. Your world has had many troubles. It will have troubles until spiritual principles are the foundation on which orders of society are built. To try and erect these on a materialistic basis is equivalent to building on quicksand. You cannot have peace without while there is war within. How can there be co-operation when hatred, violence, enmity, greed and sloth are the expressions of too many people?

Love is the fulfilling of the law. You must love one another because you recognize that every individual in your world is your spiritual brother or sister, and that the whole human family consists of spiritual kith and kin. This is what the Great Spirit has done by implanting into every being a portion of its own divinity so that the chain of the spirit in which you are all links girdles the whole of your world.

At present there is no recognition of this eternal fact that primarily you are spiritual beings none of whom can live in isolation from others; that your evolution is bound up with one another; that you advance or retreat collectively.

This is your responsibility. I have always said that knowledge brings responsibility as to how it is to be employed. Once you are aware of spiritual truths, once you are familiar with the working of the power of the spirit, you should have no fear of today or the morrow.

No harm will befall your spirit. If you live according to what you know and what has been revealed to you, you will come through unsinged, no matter what the fire. You cannot be spiritually hurt or crushed by whatever happens in your world. You have all had evidence in your own lives of what the power of the spirit can do when conditions are right.

Unfortunately those who are aware of these vital truths are the few and not the many. The majority think that power resides in matter, in force, in domination, in tyranny, in slavery. But all the children of the Great Spirit are born to be free in body, mind and spirit.

Gradually as these truths infiltrate and permeate everywhere, the children of earth will live in greater liberty and a brighter lustre will be their everyday existence. You have not come to the end of the history in this land or any other lands. The divine power of evolution will slowly and gradually reveal itself. People on earth may block, impede and delay, but they cannot alter the divine will.

If they could overcome the will of the Great Spirit then the earth would have crumbled a long time ago. Spirit is superior to matter. The divine spirit is the overruling power. I always say, lift up your hearts, hold your heads high, there is nothing to fear in your world, or in ours for that matter. You will come through.

Q *Do spirit guides approve of cremation?*

YES, always, because essentially it has the effect of putting an end to the idea that the spirit is in the physical body.

Crying

IT is good sometimes to shed tears to provide relief and to bring comfort as a result. It is better to shed tears than to have within you bottled up emotions which are unexpressed.

Difficulties and crises

DIFFICULTIES are challenges. If you had no difficulties, problems, obstacles or hindrances, there would be no opportunity for your latent powers to express themselves.

In moments of crises you become aware that you have an inner reservoir of strength on which you can call. Usually you scratch only the surface of what you can get. There is no difficulty so great that you have not the power, with the inner strength that you possess and the guidance you can receive, to triumph over it.

Q *Are all the disasters that occur on our planet within the divine plan?*

IN the sense that man cannot work outside the divine plan, because there is an inexorable law of cause and effect. The overruling law maintains the limitation that is imposed on man. Let me put it quite bluntly. Your scientists cannot devise a means of destruction that would completely destroy the whole of the universe. That is the limitation.

Divine intervention

 We hear of the sea being calm at Dunkirk and of the weather being favourable in Sicily, was this due to divine intervention?

THERE is not intervention by the Great Spirit. The laws, the universal natural laws, have always been in existence. There is no circumstance that has ever happened, or will ever happen, that requires the suspension of any natural law or the intervention in any natural law. The world is ruled by natural laws, and it is not necessary for any interference to take place.

If it were, then the Great Spirit would cease to be the Great Spirit, for, instead of being perfect, the Great Spirit would by chaotic.

Doubt as to the way

WHEN there is any doubt, withdraw into the silence where the strident noise of the physical world is stilled and your spirit can find more expression. Then as you attune yourself you will find there comes an inner peace, tranquillity, repose and resolution that will enable you to be sure that what is best for you will be revealed.

Dreams

 How can dreams be accounted for? Some of them can hardly be accepted as memories of spirit travels.

THERE are dreams and dreams. Some of them are capable of physical explanation, as they are only reflex action of a brain which is hushed for a while. Some of them are only caused by the food you eat. But beyond all these, there are dreams which are the memories of your experience in our world, which you retain in very fragmentary form. The reason why your dreams are so often distorted is that when you come to the planes of spirit you are freed from the restrictions of earth and, in the effort to remember spirit experiences in earthly limitations, you get distortion.

Drugs

 To what would you attribute the sudden increase in drug-taking and addiction, especially among young people? Can we offer any tangible aid to them?

YES, you can offer healing, the power of the spirit. This is always directed to the spirit or soul of an unfortunate being who has resorted to what could be dangerous drugs and who can be helped. You must try to realise that the power of the spirit is also the power of the Great Spirit, which is the life force.

It is the vitality, the dynamic, the mainspring of all existence. There is no life without spirit. Everybody who moves, breathes or thinks does so because of the spirit. In healing, the life force is applied to the weakened vitality of the individual whose body, mind and spirit are in disarray through the intake of certain drugs. These have caused this disharmony, and thus there is a blockage, an impediment where natural channels should be flowing freely and harmoniously with one another.

If you have the gift of healing, you are a channel for this divine power which can stimulate, in the way that you charge a depleted battery, and enable the life force to flow again, rid itself of the impediments and blockages which have brought ill-health to the individual.

This is a much greater contribution than giving the individual another drug to get rid of the previous one. As to why so many resort to drugs, this is very simple. They are in despair, they are frustrated, they are pessimistic, they see no hope for themselves, they are out of touch with reality, they have lost their spiritual way and they can find in materialism no support for them. They look to the drug to give them a lift, but it is not the way. As I said before, nature works by evolution, not by revolution.

Death

Q *How would you explain death to a child?*

IF the child has the ability to understand what is being said, of course, I would say that death is the opening of a door into a larger life, just as the cage is opened to allow the bird to be free.

Depletion of the earth's resources

Q *Do you agree that we have destroyed many things which can never be returned to what they were? This applies to much of what was in the ground and it is a limited place that we inhabit.*

BUT the Earth has tremendous potentialities. There is much to be revealed in your world, much to be discovered. You are not at the end of evolution. You are still in its early stages.

Those who are familiar with the truths of the spirit never despair. Their optimism is based on the knowledge that has been revealed to them. With that knowledge they can have complete faith in the overriding power.

In its long history your world has had many disasters. Man has survived them. Man has progressed in spite of himself. He will continue to evolve because evolution is part of the natural law. And spiritual evolution is part of that same law.

Depression for no apparent reason

Q What has come over our young people?

THEY have not found their way. They have come into a world where violence rules. They believe their elders have betrayed them. They feel also that they can obtain no guidance from conventional religion.

Q How can one help another suffering from depression?

THEY have to learn to change their outlook and to have faith built on the foundation of knowledge. Faith built on incredulity will easily vanish because it is based on shifting sands. Faith founded on knowledge will endure.

Destiny

Q What is man's ultimate destiny after the cycles of his earthly lives?

ULTIMATE destiny? I know nothing of ultimates. With beginnings and ends I cannot deal. Life is infinite; progress is infinite, too. Cycles have neither end nor beginning. Progress is infinite.

Destruction of the earth

YOUR world will not be destroyed overnight. The Great Spirit, with infinite love and wisdom, has devised natural laws which provide for every facet of being, mighty or minute, complex or simple. The natural laws operate by evolution, not revolution. They ensure that the power of man is restricted. There are things he cannot do. He has a measure of free will, but it is limited.

Development of knowledge

Q *So what I suffer now is not necessary my own fault?*

IF that brings you consolation you are welcome to the thought. I will let you into a secret. The more knowledge you have the less choice you have. Increasing knowledge unerringly dictates the part that you must play. Those of us who have volunteered to serve must serve until our missions are accomplished. You have chosen, therefore you have no choice. Knowledge can only come when you are ready to receive it. That is how the law works. I was asked to perform a mission and I undertook to do so. The fact that you have invited me to come and talk with you shows that to some extent I may have succeeded in relaying the wisdom of others whose mouthpiece it is my privilege to be. There is a spiritual relationship that endures when the physical relationship has ended. The spiritual relationship is eternal. What binds is not matter but spirit. Matter is ephemeral, spirit is eternal.

Q *Are not the experiences on this earth – such as war, pain, mental and physical suffering, disease, sorrow, love, hate, joy and happiness – essential for the development and progress of mankind and a part of the divine plan?*

NO, they are not. Wars are not made by the Great Spirit. Disease is not given by the Great Spirit. These are the things that the children of matter have brought upon themselves by the misuse of their free will. There are lessons to be learned, but they can be learned without the brutalities and the hideous cruelties that the children of the Great Spirit perpetrate against each other. Do not mistake the doings of man for the acts of the Great Spirit.

Earthly life's purpose

THE whole object of earthly life is to have a variety of experiences that will fit the spirit for the next stage beyond earth when you have to pass into our world. That is why you come to earth in the first place. Earth is the training ground, the school where the spirit learns its lessons which will provide its equipment for the life beyond earth.

For that reason I say to you again that what you regard as the bad experiences can be the best ones for you. It is not in the sunshine that the soul finds itself, but in the storm. It is when the thunder rages and the lightning flashes.

You must be sharpened, purged, refined. You must experience the heights and the depths. You must have the variety of experiences that earth provides for you. In this way the spirit emerges stronger, fortified, ready for what awaits it when death comes.

The object of all earthly existence is that the human spirit is to be quickened. The essence of life on earth is it offers stark contrast and polarities. It provides goodness and the lack of goodness. This does not obtain in our world, where each sphere does not have this contrast.

The object of earthly life is to make available a variety of experiences to enable the soul to exercise its divine potential, and emerge stronger as a result. And so you will have crimes, sin and violence.

The object of all earthly existence is that the human spirit, the divine element in all mankind and animals, and indeed in all life, is to be quickened so what is only a spark can become a flickering light, and gradually a beauteous flame. Self-fulfilment begins, and people in your world are able to enjoy what life, not only on its surface but in its more important inner aspects, has to offer them.

Q *What is the object of earthly life?*

THE whole object is that you shall realise what you are. You are meant to give full expression to the body and the spirit. It is equally wrong to think only of spiritual things and neglect your physical obligations as it is to concentrate on the purely physical requirements and neglect your spiritual duties. There should be a perfect balance, so that you can be in the world but not of the world; that your physical body should be cared for, because it is the temple of the divine spirit, and that the spirit, which is in the process of growth and evolution, shall have opportunities for expressing growth and evolution through the body.

Q *What is the use of man's earthly experience, bearing in mind it is so limited in comparison with eternity?*

ETERNITY is the sum total of an infinite number of experiences. In eternity, every experience, every action, word and thought plays its part, however small it may be. Eternity is the result of all these accumulated experiences, and if one is lacking then there is not a complete balance. In a vast orchestra of two or three hundred players the man who sounds the triangle, regarded perhaps as the most insignificant instrumentalist, has an important part to play, for if when his time comes he strikes the wrong note, or if he fails to add his sound to the volume, then the whole symphony would be distorted. You realise that. So it is with your earthly lives. It is part, and an essential part, of the training of the soul, and your soul will register indelibly for ever the marks of that training.

Evil

Q *If evil is due to man's misuse of his free will, then why should the Great Spirit endow him with that free will which He knows would be misused?*

HOW else could you have man fulfilling his destiny? Not all are evil, to use that word. There is a mixture in mankind. If you have to choose between a puppet, an automaton, and a being with potential powers of selfishness and saintliness, which would you prefer? Would you prefer man to participate in the infinite processes of creation? If so, he must have virtues and faults, for without the faults he could not have the virtues. Life is comparative. Man rises through struggle and difficulty; man attains, because attainment is not easy, but because it is hard, and that process refines the soul, purifies his nature and makes his character grow. Darkness is where light is not; evil is where good is not; ignorance is where knowledge is not. If all the world were good, it would cease to be good. If all the world had knowledge, it would cease to be knowledge. If all the world had light, it would cease to be light. You grow through comparative experiences. You achieve the heights because you have tasted the depths. That which is achieved without struggled is lightly prized. That which is achieved with struggle is counted as an endearing prize.

 Would you say that something which appears evil from the human standpoint may not be evil at all – in fact from a higher standpoint it might be regarded as good?

TO many people in your world suffering is evil, pain is unwelcome, but this is not necessarily the case. Pain is just as much a part of the divine plan as pleasure. Without pain there could be no pleasure, without darkness there could be no light, without hatred there could be no love. Action and reaction are equal and opposite. They are the two sides of the same coin. Good and evil are fundamental and comparative. You have codes of morality in your world dependant on the place where you live. But it is not the same code of morality in every place. Our evaluation is based upon the effect on the soul. This is the important thing, anything which advances soul-attainment is good; anything which retards soul-attainment is bad.

Fabric of the etheric

Q Does the fabric of the etheric country have a material core, of which the earth is a local example?

AM I material? Is love between men and women material? Is the inspiration of an artist material? Is the appreciation of music material? The answer to these questions depends on what you call material. If you mean is it real, does it possess reality, then I say yes, for the spirit is the greatest reality of life, and that which you call material, the world of matter, is but the shell which surrounds the reality.

Fear

PERFECT love casteth out fear. Knowledge dispels fear, for fear is born of ignorance. Where there is love and trust and knowledge, there fear cannot reign. An evolved spirit cannot be afraid at any time, because he knows that there is no experience that can come to him in any phase of life that he cannot master, for he is the Great Spirit.

Fear creates its own prison for the soul. You must learn to rise above fear and not allow its vibrations to hinder you, to have perfect faith and confidence and trust, to know that you can stand on your own feet and say: "I am the Great Spirit and the wind of circumstance cannot shake me. I will rise triumphant over every difficulty because of the infinite power which is within my soul". You have power over every circumstance. Would you limit the power of the infinite soul?

Never allow fear to find lodgement within your being. It is a negative quality which destroys, vitiates and saps. It impairs your judgement; it clouds your reason; it prevents you from seeing issues clearly. There is no problem that comes to any soul which you are incapable of solving. There is no difficulty that you cannot conquer — if you would but allow the latent divinity to rise to the surface.

Freedom

Q *What do you mean by freedom?*

I VIEW all questions in the light of the experience of the spirit. I see man as a spirit striving to express himself through a body, and I see millions with that spirit stifled, crushed, repressed and trampled on. True freedom does not mean the right of every individual to do as he pleases, the right to follow every whim, caprice or inclination. Freedom involves responsibility and understanding of the purpose for which human beings have been placed in your world.

Free will and dependence on karma

THE whole of life is regulated by natural laws. Nothing is left to freakishness, to miracles or to chance. All is cause and effect, sowing and reaping, otherwise the universe would be chaotic. You have evidence of an infinite plan, of an infinite intelligence in the natural laws wherever you look.

It is to be seen in the sequence of the seasons, the movements of planets and galaxies, the ebb and flow of tides, the growth of a myriad forms of floral life, where natural law rules supreme. So there is the limit which the divine power has placed because nothing can occur beyond the framework of natural law. But there are laws within laws. There are not only physical laws, there are mental and spiritual ones.

It is part of the plan that you should have an element of free will, the power and ability to make choices in certain circumstances. Used for its best and highest, you can play your part in the spiritual unfoldment and evolution of the race, the world, the universe and the cosmos because your spirit is part of the Great Spirit.

You share in the divinity that is responsible for all that exists everywhere. You are the Great Spirit in microcosm. All that the Great Spirit has of that infinity you have and you will have infinity in which to unfold it.

You can wake up tomorrow morning at an hour earlier or an hour later, or you can stay in bed if you like. You can go for a walk or drive a car. You can lose your temper and hope to find it again. There is a variety of things you can do for which you have free will.

But you cannot stop the sun from shining, you cannot halt the tempest; these are beyond your power. Your free will is limited because your choice is restricted. There is another limitation placed on your free will. It is the mental and spiritual stage you have reached in your development. You are free to kill, but your character will ensure that you refrain. So that when you have choices you are limited by who and what you are at the time. Like many things in the universe you have a paradox. You have free will within limitations all the time.

Now I must go a stage further because you introduced the question of karma. This, too, is a very important consideration because many of those that have work to do in your world chose to do it beforehand. Though awareness may not come immediately, the choice imposes another restriction on free will.

Free will, does it exist?

IT is part of the complementary aspect of the law that man and woman help to make the whole. Intuition can help where reason cannot give the answer. You are being given the opportunity to fulfil yourselves. You have free will. You may make the choice.

Life is not chance, accident or even coincidence. The whole of life is governed by immutable natural law. Whatever aspect of being you examine, it is due to natural law. Human beings are not outside the operation of natural law. They are integral parts of it.

The law has operated at a time when you have a choice to make. It is for you to make that choice. You have been led by those who love you. It is love that directs your footsteps. And that love is capable of guiding you if you will allow it to do so.

Love, like life, is indestructible. The things of matter must perish because by their very nature they are ephemeral. The things of the spirit are eternal. Love is a quality of the spirit. Love endures, love survives, love, as your Bible says, is the fulfilling of the law.

 After replying at length to a question on the part played by spirit guidance and that played by our own efforts, Silver Birch was asked: You said there were times when you had to stand back and let those you love make their choice. They had free will to go which way they liked. What happens if they throw spanners into the works?

THERE is free will up to a point, but it is never a free free will. It is a free will that is conditioned and restricted by certain circumstances of spiritual growth and evolution. It is not a complete and unfettered free will in which you have perfect liberty of choice.

 Is there no such thing as free will?

THERE is a free will within certain limits – you can choose which path you take at a certain moment and either hinder or advance your spiritual progress.

 Whilst you do that, surely you may be hindering or advancing someone else?

THAT is possible. But may I try to explain, if I can, that on the surface all is simple. Behind the surface there are highly complex workings because there are laws within laws, within laws, within laws. Such, however, is the perfection of the Great Spirit's wisdom that all is balanced to an extent that the operation cannot fail.

Q *Isn't it possible that the spanner that we might throw in the works isn't important enough to have much effect on the total plan?*

YOU can throw a spanner and injure some of the works, but you cannot throw a spanner into all the works. The damage you can do is comparatively small. Nobody in your world has the means at his or her disposal to wreck completely the will of the Great Spirit, or to do the amount of damage that could prevent the divine plan from operating.

Free will

IT is the way you settle your problems that develops what is within you. You do not develop the spirit when everything is easy and smooth, but when you have difficulties. But there are times when we feel justified in interfering with your judgement. I would interfere if a very vital principle were involved. If it meant that my work through my medium would be interrupted, then I would interfere so that the channel would still be free. But where the problems only involve my medium's own evolution, then they are his responsibility and he must work them out for himself.

Different faiths

Q *What is your opinion about our connection with different faiths? Should we tolerate those who try to infiltrate our truths? Or should we go our path alone and estrange ourselves from them, as some people want to do? In my view knowledge of Spiritualism should be infiltrated into the churches, tolerating their activity. Spiritualism should help those with little faith to become more religious.*

QUESTIONS & ANSWERS

THESE are words that you use, like Spiritualism, but we are not concerned with words. Words are an attempt to clothe ideas and realities. We are concerned that the Power of the spirit, of God – use your own words but I call it the Great Spirit – shall make a lodgement in your world wherever it can. That is the purpose behind everything that we do. Why do we want the power of the spirit to effect a lodgement? So that it can touch souls and bring them into life. It does not matter where this is done, in a church, outside a church, or in a home. It is the individual soul that should be touched, wherever you can reach it.

Those who are ready to be awakened out of their materialistic sleep will come into your orbit, or you can go to them and try to plant the seed of the spirit. If you fail, shed a silent tear – not for yourself, but for them. They have had the opportunity and alas they have not taken it. But here and there the seed will fall into the ground that is receptive. And it will begin to grow, to flower and to burgeon into beauty and grace because it is the seed of divinity. Then the soul is beginning to come into its own.

The whole purpose of earthly life is that man should live on all aspects of being, physically, mentally and spiritually, and until these three are functioning he is not fulfilling himself. If he is living only with his body and mind, he is chasing illusion and shadow and missing reality. But when the soul begins to come into its own, it opens the door to tremendous spiritual possibilities and adventures for him. That is why he incarnates into your world of matter so that the soul should come into its own.

So it is not important that it should happen in this or that place, but only that it should happen. This is the reason for pain and suffering in your world, so that the individual should reach that crisis when matter can offer him no more and he is ready to turn to the spirit. "The wind bloweth where it listeth", as it says in your Bible. Let the wind blow where it will. Where you meet with receptivity, help as much as you can.

Future of the world

YOUR world will continue to exist because there is no individual or combination of individuals who have the power to destroy the whole of it. There is a limitation placed upon the harm that can be done and the means that you can use, or can be invented or discovered, to wreak damage on such a vast scale that the world would cease to be tenable.

Greed and power

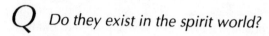

GREED and power still exist in what may be called the lower astral spheres. What you must realise is that spiritually an individual is exactly the same one day after death as he was before it. Our world, unlike yours, is one where thought is reality. What you think is real and substantial.

The trouble is that lust for power and greed chain (them) to earth. Though materially dead, they are spiritually dead as well. They are nearer to your world than they are to us. Unfortunately they can harm those like themselves in your world who are concerned only with greed and power.

Spirit guides

Q Do they enter the bodies of a medium in order to speak?

NO, not always. In most cases he works through the aura of the medium.

Q Do they utilize the vocal organs of the medium?

SOMETIMES. I am using this medium's vocal organs now. If I desired, I could build my own, but that is a waste of power. I take control of the subconscious part of the medium, which gives me control of all his bodily organs. I displace his will, which he has agreed I should do, and, for the time being, I am in charge of his body. When I have done my work, I retire from his aura and his consciousness returns to pick up the threads once again.

Q *Do you have to displace the medium's spirit body during control?*

SOMETIMES I do, but it is always connected with the earthly body.

Q *Spirit guides – separate entities or extensions of one's own personality?*

IT is a rather complex subject. I would prefer to use the word "individuality" rather than "personality", which is physical, and the individuality which is the soul or spiritual make up, the reality behind the mask, so to speak.

Persons are persons so far as your world is concerned, but you cannot separate spiritual individuality in the same way. There are, for example, affinities, two kindred halves of the one soul, and sometimes they incarnate at the same time.

There are also what I call facets of the one diamond. This is the oversoul, the greater individuality, and the facets are aspects of it which incarnate into your world for experience that will add lustre to the diamond when they return to it.

Also there are people who, although separate persons, are aspects of the one individuality. For instance, my medium, his wife and myself are parts of one individual. So you can have facets of the one guide. You can call these extensions if you like, but it comes to the same thing. Only one infinitesimal part of the whole individuality can be manifested in physical form on earth.

Q *Does every human being have a spirit guide?*

FROM the moment of conception and even before that, there is attached to the incarnating soul someone who volunteers to act as his guardian. "He has given His angels charge concerning thee, to keep thee in Thy ways" is a literal truth. The guardian will maintain to the best of his or her ability the function assumed until the time comes for you to cross the border. The task becomes easier when you are aware of the guardianship; it becomes difficult when you are unaware of it. There is only one guide, but many helpers. The guardian angel knows before he assumes his task what lies ahead of him and does not have a free choice in the matter either. Not everyone can say I will be the guardian to this or that person. Ours is a very organised world.

Q *Who appoints spirit guides?*

THE law of attraction.

Q *We are told that everybody has a guardian angel. If so, why should some guardian angels be unable to protect those in their care from harm and to keep them safe while others apparently are able to so?*

IT is all governed by the circumstances of the time. It is true that everybody has a guardian angel in one form or another, but how many realise this fact? Where there is no realisation, unless the individual is unconsciously psychic, then the guide or spirit being is unable to register in your world.

The whole activity of the spirit is dependent upon your providing the conditions through which it can express itself. When you provide the conditions, a finely-attuned instrument in harmony with the world of spirit, then those who are close to you can manifest their presence and make their impact on matter. That explains all the cases of guardianship, protection and guidance, of which you have many records. It is for you to provide the right conditions. You are our hands, without them we cannot work in your world.

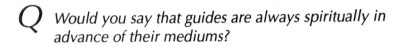

Q Would you say that guides are always spiritually in advance of their mediums?

NO, I would not. It depends upon the task that has to be performed and it also depends upon the construction that you give to the word "guide". Those in our world who are associated with earthly instruments work in co-operation. There is usually a band attached to each medium, and there is at the head the directing intelligence. He is the one who should be more properly described as the guide, for the rest are working under his direction and although, occasionally, some of them may speak through the medium, they do so only at the request of the one in charge. But their functioning is not quite the same. That is why you sometimes use the word "control" to mark the difference between two kinds of beings who manifest through mediums.

If you refer to the usual method that is employed in the case of trance mediums, then it is always true that the guide in charge is the spiritual superior of the medium. But in certain physical plenomena, many of those employed in the group to accomplish results need not be of great spiritual attainment. In fact, some of them can best fulfil their function because of their proximity to earthly conditions, and in such cases it is true to say that the members of the spirit band are not necessarily more spiritually advanced than the medium that is used. But it is true in the general sense of the guide that is the controlling, directing influence and the medium, otherwise the initiative could not very well come from our side.

Hatred

HATRED is never right. It is wrong to hate. You must love. You must even try to love those who hate you and those who would do their worst to you. You must love in its most compassionate form. The acme of spiritual healing, for example, is compassionate love. Without compassion, healing exists only in its physical or magnetic state. With compassion the spirit power is beginning to operate and there is love in action. This is the divine, the Great Spirit has been reflected in the service that you render. We must try to supplant hatred with love because this is transforming darkness into light.

Hauntings

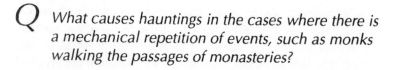 *What causes hauntings in the cases where there is a mechanical repetition of events, such as monks walking the passages of monasteries?*

SOME hauntings are caused by spirits, but in the cases you mention they are caused by intense concentration on earth, leaving an etheric picture which can still be registered. Usually, however, that which your world calls a ghost is one we recognise as an earthbound spirit.

Holy Trinity

Q When speaking of the trinity, the questioner said "I find it all very confusing".

So do I. Give your allegiance to the truth as revealed to you. To believe in the unbelievable is no credit to your intelligence. Neither will it help your soul to grow.

Hypnotic regression – evidence of past life or spirit control?

IT can be sometimes, in what is called regression, that a contact is made with a previous physical existence, but it is not always the case that this occurs. The mind's potential is so vast that none in your world has fathomed all its recesses. It is creative, it has subconscious desires, it can lend itself to temporary spirit possession.

All these factors have to be taken into account. There can be what you call astral projection and the impingement of a series of events which are recorded in the hypnotic trance. This does not mean that the subject is necessarily expressing a past incarnation.

Infant prodigies

Q Will you explain infant prodigies?

THERE are three kinds. Some are incarnated souls with a memory of past experiences to help. Others are mediums subject to spirit influence, albeit unconsciously, and therefore receptacles of much learning, wisdom, knowledge and truth from our world. The others are geniuses who are advanced guards of evolution.

Insecticides

Q Is it wrong to spray with insecticides to try to prevent malaria, sleeping sickness, etc?

OF course you must have respect for all life, but this is a question of motive and degree. If you have conditions where, due to certain circumstances, there are the kind of insects that cause disease, then your motive for using sprays is a good one. Respect for life must be tempered with the necessity of ensuring there are conditions in which it can flourish. Similarly if you have houses infested with bugs, it is easier to spray and get rid of them if your motive is to improve the health of those who dwell there.

Intuition – spirit prompting

Intuition is the means by which the spirit becomes aware of itself; it outpaces the processes of normal earthly reasoning. Intuition accomplishes at lightning speed what normally you would reach after much deliberation. Intuition is that process of attunement during which you receive that prompting which you would reach after much time and thought on the same subject.

Individuality

 Another question that crops up many times is the thought of returning to God. There is a certain fear that you lose your individuality in this return.

THE ultimate is not attainment of Nirvana. All spiritual progress is towards increasing individuality. You do not become less of an individual, you become more of an individual. You develop latent gifts, you acquire greater knowledge, your character becomes stronger, more of the divine is exhibited through you. The Great Spirit is infinite and so there is an infinite development to be achieved. Perfection is never attained, there is a constant striving towards it. You do not ever lose yourself. What you succeed in doing is finding yourself.

Is it possible to describe this state we are supposed to reach?

NO, because you get to conditions and spheres that are beyond language. They consist of states of consciousness and awareness. This is something you will not understand until you attain it. You do not lose your individuality in a sea of greater consciousness, but that depth of the ocean becomes included in your individuality.

Would it be that the individuality is part of the personality, or is it the other way round?

IT is the personality that is the fragment of the individuality.

Killing

Q *To what extent is man allowed to kill?*

I DON'T like the use of the word "allowed". Mankind is given free will, but in a measure that is qualified and restricted. It is not an unfettered free will enabling individuals to do everything they would like to do. The bestowal of free will is part of the divine plan so that people have the opportunity of co-operating, of living in harmony with the natural laws, the infinite processes of creation, and achieving health, understanding, realisation and fulfilment. Killing is wrong, though there are qualifications. Because you have not the power to confer life, then you should not have the power to end it. There are qualifications because there are other considerations to be met. The more you evolve spiritually the more you realise that you must act in accordance with clear principles that are based on a knowledge of spiritual realities.

Q *Do you think we should let a bully kill innocent people?*

YOU want us to pronounce a verdict on halfway happenings, but we deal with eternal principles. If the eternal principles had been applied in the beginning, then you would not have your present difficulties. Because you have reached difficulties, you say to us: Shall we apply some measure which may, for the moment, remedy the evil which has accrued? Only eternal principles can procure eternal peace.

How is the inflicter of capital punishment, such as a hangman or the operator of an electric chair, judged when he reaches the spirit world?

IF he knows it is wrong, he will pay the penalty for sinning with knowledge. If he does not know it is wrong, then there will be no punishment.

Knowledge and faith

IT says in your Bible "add to your faith knowledge". I say when you have knowledge, add faith to it. You cannot have all knowledge. You are human, restricted in your capacity, for your reception is of necessity limited.

The foundation of knowledge should be your base to enable you to withstand all the storms and tempests of earthly life, to be unshaken no matter what happens. Let your faith help you where your knowledge cannot take you.

Leisure

THE right use of leisure should be devoted to the cultivation of the gifts of the mind and of the spirit. That is important, for already most people devote sufficient time to the requirements of the physical body. They concern themselves with the food that is required to sustain them and give them energy, although they are not always cognisant of those laws of health which would enable the body to be the vital organism it should be. But few remember that the mind and the spirit require development, and these are the ones who go through life spiritually deaf, dumb and blind.

Can you say something about the right use of leisure?

THAT is a very good question (answer as above). The vast, inexhaustible riches of the spirit are unknown to them. The beauty which could fill their mind and spirit has not yet been made known to them. They know little of the many arts, the cultivation of which would bring them inner peace and a greater appreciation of the larger side of life.

Then, above all, is the cultivation of the spirit itself which can be accomplished in the quietness of the individual, where he can learn to attune himself to all that power that is round and about him; where he can learn to harmonise his mind with the great minds of the larger life; where he can learn to become a better receptacle for the inspiration and wisdom, for the knowledge and truth, for all the learning that is awaiting him from the infinite storehouse, the Great Spirit.

Loneliness

YOU feel lonely. Every soul treading the path of attainment must experience loneliness. But you have the companionship of evolved beings who will never desert you. Your strength comes not from your world but from ours.

 If a person is compelled to live a life of loneliness on this earth, is he compelled to lead that life after death?

OH no. The law is always perfect. The soul reaps its own reward and makes its own punishment. Those who are attracted by love and affection will meet because their souls will throw them together on that plane.

Love and marriage

Q *In the spirit life, do we join again with those we love and become younger? Jesus says there is no marriage or giving in marriage.*

WHENEVER there has been love between a man and a woman and that love has brought them together and made them as one, and they have lived on the same spiritual plane in your world, then "death" will not part them. "Death" will be a door which will give them a greater freedom for their souls to be more closely united than they were in your world of matter.

But if their coming together, their marriage as you call it, was not a marriage of souls but only of bodies, and their souls did not dwell on the same plane, then "death" will drive them further apart, for it will relegate them to their own spiritual spheres. If there is love they will find that in the world of spirit they will not get younger, not younger, but will experience growth, evolution, development. These are things of the soul, not the body.

When the Nazarene said that there was no marriage and no giving in marriage, he was referring to the marriage of bodies, not the marriage of souls. For that which you call male and that which you call female each has its contribution to make to each other. The female is necessary to the male and the male is necessary to the female. The Great Spirit embodies the two principles in perfection. As you evolve in the planes of spirit the differences become less and less.

Lower planes

Q *What will be the position of those who, after passing, go to the lower planes of spirit life? Will they remember their sleep visits, presumably to the lower planes, and will that memory help them to adjust to their position?*

THOSE who would gravitate to the lower planes go to those planes during sleep, but the memory of that would not help them to realise their position after death because the planes on which they found themselves would still resemble the material world.

The lower in the world of spirit, the more earthly it is in appearance because the vibrations are more gross; the higher in the realm of spirit, the finer the vibrations.

Man's destructiveness

YOUR world is at a precarious stage in its evolution. It is almost seemingly a touch and go situation. You will come through. Pay no heed to the Cassandras, to the prophets and criers of woe.

The Great Spirit has placed a limit on the damage and the harm that can be done by man in your world. There is no power in your world that is able to destroy the whole of it. There is no power that can kill the physical bodies of all who dwell in it. There is a limit to what man can do with the most complicated, efficient technological devices he can invent.

The power of the spirit is stronger than any power of matter that can be produced. Matter is inferior to spirit. Spirit is king and matter is servant. Spirit is supreme, matter exists only because of spirit operating through it. When spirit withdraws, matter disintegrates. Spirit is the overruling power to ensure that you will come through.

Man's place in the scheme of things

YOU are part of the eternal process of life. Because you consider that man is a higher species than other forms of life, you have a responsibility to help what you regard as the lower, just as you desire that higher beings in our world should help you.

Matter

MATTER is by its very nature ephemeral, transient. It has no permanence in the form that is physically manifested. Anything material exists only because it is given life by the spirit. It is the spirit which is the dynamic, the vivifying power that enables you and everything else in your world to live. When the spirit withdraws, matter crumbles. Your body returns to the dust, but you, the spirit, continue on your eternal path of progress.

Materialisation

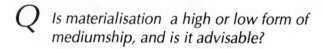 *Is materialisation a high or low form of mediumship, and is it advisable?*

ANYTHING which brings to one soul happiness or knowledge of the laws of the spirit has served its purpose. Do not think in terms of high or low. Think in terms of service to those who need it.

Mediumistic excellence

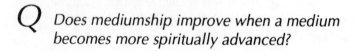 *Does mediumship improve when a medium becomes more spiritually advanced?*

ALWAYS, the higher the life the greater the mediumship. There is nothing worthwhile to be achieved unless you are prepared to sacrifice. Isn't that what all of us who return to your world have to learn?

Mental revolution – spirit organised?

YOUR world is in a melting pot. You are seeing the war between good and evil, similar to the story told in the Bible. You are also seeing the unfortunate results of the worship of mammon, the pursuit of greed and avarice, the desire for material power, the subjection of all that is noble, elevating, spiritual; the selfishness that I call the festering cancer of your world.

At the same time religion, in its conventional sense, has lost its potency, influence and validity to guide and direct. Allegiance to false doctrines that make no sense to those that have intelligence means that an increasing number continue to turn their backs on what the conventional religions have to offer.

Mistakes

 Are we making serious mistakes in our approach to the world in general? If we are, could you enlighten us on these mistakes?

IF you never made mistakes, you would not be on earth. That is why you are there, to make mistakes and to learn from them. If you were perfect, there would be no need to incarnate. You are there so that you can learn, and that is part of the law of evolution. But evolution is not a finite process, it is an infinite one. The object of evolution is growth towards perfection. But perfection is infinite and cannot be achieved. It has been achieved only by the Great Spirit, who is infinite love and infinite wisdom. The more perfect you become the more you will realise there is further perfection to be attained. It is not a static process.

The law of evolution is working itself out through all its manifold stages and these are happening concurrently. Man's physical evolution, despite what scientists say, is not yet over. It has many forms yet to be expressed. Similarly, the mental and spiritual evolutions have a long way to go, even on earth, before they attain the stage which they should reach as part of the three-fold purpose of man's incarnation.

You must recognise that this is an endless process in your world and in the whole universe in itself evidence of the infinite intelligence which has devised the whole scheme, with wondrous laws that never fail and which provide for every facet of being everywhere to be guided, sustained and regulated. All of us are within this scheme of infinite love, law and wisdom. So go on making mistakes, learning from them and getting better spiritually all the time.

Morality and immorality

WHAT is meant by immoral? Some things you regard as moral we would regard as highly immoral. It depends on your outlook. To me morality is that ideal which infuses you always with the idea of acting always according to the highest principles of which you are aware. This is to be kind, helpful and compassionate.

It is not to inflict hurt or injury to another; not in any way to impede the progress of another, to do nothing that causes you shame or a later knowledge that you have behaved in a fashion that is inconsistent with the truths you have received.

That is the morality I understand, that I would teach to others. As to whether your world is more or less moral must depend on your interpretation of morality. In some respects it is essentially, economically and spiritually better; in others it is not so because evolution does not move in a straight line.

New Age

TO me there is a constant process of evolution, development, unfoldment. It will not happen that over night there will be change and a new age will be ushered in. Gradually, as truth progresses, more and more people will become aware of it. Once they realise that the whole of the universe is founded on spiritual realities that cannot fail, and as a result they begin to live these implications, so there will be higher states of consciousness and awareness functioning in your world, but it will be a gradual process.

The New Testament

[Silver Birch was asked to comment on certain texts of the New Testament.]

I AM not going to be tied down by words which appear in your Bible. As I have said so many times, they are not an accurate representation of what transpired in those days.

Neither do I regard it as fitting or appropriate that my ability to teach truth should depend on my ability to illumine or interpret texts from the Bible. What I have to say must stand or fall by its own reasonableness, by my ability, if it be an ability, to expound the truth in such a way that it will be acceptable to those who hear, read or learn it. That is all that I claim to do. I do not claim to be one who will expound the gospels. These matters, interesting though they may be, are incidental. Let us not be deviated from our main task; let us not be sidetracked; let us keep to the fundamentals of truths received in your own day and generation which you are capable of testing for yourselves. And let us all rejoice that the voice of the spirit is once again heard in the land and that the Great Spirit continues to reveal Himself to all those who have eyes to see and ears with which to hearken.

Nuclear power

I DO not regard your nuclear power as evil. The use made of it can be evil. On the other hand, the use that can be made of it could be of tremendous benefit to your world. The decision lies with those who are capable of directing or misdirecting this tremendous power.

Peace

Q Do you agree with the Pacifist movement?

I BELONG to no party. I wear no label. I see service, motive. Do not be confused with titles. Ask what is the aim, what is the desire, because there are men of good intent even in opposing camps. The teaching that we have to give you is very simple, but it requires courage to put it into practice. Whenever a start is made, whenever there is the determination that comes with knowledge of the spirit and the truths of the spirit, whenever service and not selfishness is applied to all the affairs of everyday life in the world of matter, then you will have peace and concord in your world. It will not come through any party, but through the children of the Great Spirit who, realising these things are true, apply them in their lives, in their politics, in their factories, in their governments, in their international transactions. We can enunciate principles that we know are founded on truth, and tell you with certainty that their application will bring results. You are in the world of matter. Yours is the responsibility. We can only strive to guide you, with all our love and helpfulness and co-operate with you whenever your feet are on the right paths.

[The following reply was given in a discussion of post-war conditions and the advancement of peace.]

PEACE on earth can come only when earthly individuals earn it by living lives of service, co-operation and toleration, and have good will for one another. It is not to be found by the aggrandisement of selfishness, by the few enjoying the luxuries and pleasures while they deny simple necessities to the many. Peace will come and dwell amongst you when all over the world mankind desires to live in peace and all members of the human family remember their divine origin and realise that they are knit together in an eternal fellowship of the spirit. If they build their systems on the foundations of this knowledge, then truly there will be peace.

Q *Will man ever live a life of peace with his fellows instead of warring?*

THAT is very difficult to answer. What you must appreciate is that the Great Spirit endowed man with an element of free will. Human beings could have been created as puppets. That free will provides man with the opportunity of helping what I call the infinite process of creation.

Man has the chance to make the world in which he lives a garden of Eden, a paradise, a heaven, just as he can make it a dark, desolate and grim forbidding world. That is the measure of his choice.

You have war, violence, greed, cupidity, selfishness, because materialism predominates. Materialism exists because the vast majority of people in your world do not realise there is a world beyond physical death, despite the teachings of the many religions.

Millions do not accept the fact of an inevitable after-life which is really tangible, where there is compensation and retribution. They believe that earth is the only life they will ever have. So logically they argue that if the physical is all, let us have the best it has to offer. This is the cause of war. This leads people to hate, subjugate, to imprison and even kill each other.

That is not the whole of the picture. I have paid tribute to the infallibility of the natural law which also places a restriction on the havoc that man can wreak in your world.

Perfection

Q *What is the best way to achieve a perfect state of society?*

I AM above all parties. I hold to eternal principles. Let this spirit truth be the leaven. Let it work its influence among people of all parties, of all religions, of no religion. No one group of people possesses the whole of truth; no human being, by virtue of his humanity, can contain the whole of truth. What this great knowledge can do is to teach the children of the Great Spirit who are living in your world how they can realise, not only their own potential divinities, but be the instruments for a larger power that can influence all mankind. If through millions of instruments this mighty power of the spirit could flow with all its regenerative force, bringing in its train inspiration, beauty, love and fellowship, see how every aspect of human life would be transformed. Individuals would become conscious of their imperfections and seek so to improve their own lives that they would become nearer to perfection. They would bend their energies in those directions wherever there are obstacles, impediments to man achieving the fruits of his own soul.

Thus, gradually, the whole of society would become less and less imperfect and grow nearer and nearer to perfection as all the excrescences, the blots, the stains, the hideousness were driven out and mankind lived in peace and harmony, having learnt the value of co-operation and mutual service.

Q *Perfection – can we attain it?*

IN the nature of the case, perfection cannot be attained because the question would be what happens after you attain it, when you reach the stage where you have nothing more to achieve? Perfection is an infinite process. It is the constant elimination of dross to allow the pure gold of the spirit to emerge. You cannot put a period to infinity; you cannot put a full stop to eternity.

It is like knowledge. The more you learn, the more you learn there is to be learned. You cannot arrive at the summit of all knowledge. There is an infinite number of planes, levels or spheres, of consciousness. This is an attribute of the spirit which, being infinite, means there will always be a constant development.

Obsession

 Does it mean that when a person is obsessed, the intruding spirit has received the permission of the spirit of the person obsessed? (See also "Protection of the body during sleep".)

NO, but the person obsessed has created within himself the conditions that make obsession possible. It is all a question of the individual. It is the same as when you are filled with a desire for love and service you attract those higher ones who can use you. It is the same law. The law does not work only for good. It also works the other way. All laws which can be used for the greatest service can also be abused, for as high as you can rise so low can you sink. As low as you can fall, so correspondingly can you rise to the heights. It is the same law. It depends on the way you choose to apply yourselves to it.

Obstructions to development

IF you are hurt, it seems that there still some room for development. Do not allow any thoughts of any kind from any source to hinder, mar or delay the service that you can render. You have been endowed with a gift. Use it wherever you can.

Opportunity to help and be of service

WHEN there is a desire to serve, the opportunities will be provided, but do not be in a hurry. The criticism I have to make of many people in your world is that once they become aware of spiritual realities, and that has taken a long time, they are anxious to unfold whatever gifts they possess. The way will be shown. Pray for guidance.

Past

THE only value of the past is that it is the pattern of the present and the future. It has lessons to teach. It is part of the tapestry of earthly life. All its threads play their part in forming a pattern which will emerge and show it is based on a unity and harmony of purpose.

Paths

Q Do all paths lead to God; the same place?

THE word "place" is difficult. If I put it my way, all paths lead to the one great divine source of creation. The Great Spirit, what you call "God", is infinite. So there must be an infinite number of paths leading to the Great Spirit, the epitome of perfect love and wisdom.

The Great Spirit is life, and life is spirit. All that is endowed with life has the quality of divinity as part of its heritage of birth. And all the beings who inhabit your planet are engaged on an eternal pilgrimage, pursuing paths that must, in the ultimate, lead to the one divine goal.

It does not matter what the path is as long as the pilgrim treads it with honesty of purpose, sincerely seeking to fulfil himself, acquit himself and express those gifts with which he has been endowed so that others may be enriched by his presence on earth.

Passing on, believing death is the end

AS you cannot die, because it is contrary to the natural law, the person [believing death is the end] will have to wake up and face the fact. How long it will take for the realisation of spirit life to come to him will depend upon the evolution of his soul, how far it is advanced and how it can attune itself to the new conditions.

Passing on, without understanding

AWAKENING only comes when realisation dawns. If you have knowledge, then your awakening is much quicker. We have to fight ignorance, misunderstanding, superstition, false creeds, erroneous theologies, all of which do not help to prepare the soul for its new life. Before these are conquered, the soul has gradually to accustom itself and there is a long period of rest.

As in your world you have hospitals for bruised and injured bodies, we have to treat bruised and injured souls. But where an individual has rendered great service, and love, good will, affection and prayer accompany his passing into my world, then the awakening is speeded, for all those vibrations help him.

Personality

PERSONALITY is the mask that you wear for your earthly existence. When earthly existence is over the mask is discarded.

Permissiveness

I AM in favour of people being permissive as long as they permit themselves to do the right thing. You are all endowed with a divine monitor. You call it conscience. It tells you when you are right or wrong.

Physical body

THE physical body, from the moment it is born, begins to die. Nothing can change that fact. It is not conceived to achieve permanence in your world. By nature it knows that it has only an ephemeral existence. It must follow the cycle. Gradually, it achieves the maturity of physical well being. Then just as gradually every aspect of the body begins to wear out. What should happen is that the physical body drops away, as I have said many times, when it is ripe, as the apple drops from the tree.

We in our world are not perfect. We have not attained the end of our spiritual progress. We have a long, long, way to go. But we utilise what power we can attract when we are confronted with material conditions which make it very difficult for us to work in your world.

I have always said, and will continue to say, we do not possess all knowledge because it is infinite. You in your world are able to have only a smaller amount of knowledge because you are encumbered with physical limitations that do not apply to us.

Physical phenomena, why hard to attain?

BECAUSE there is a law not only of physical evolution but of spiritual evolution. The climate of opinion has changed in your world. The physical phenomena were necessary at a time when spiritual realities had to be materially demonstrated. Scientists were not prepared to accept anything that did not come within this category.

Now your world has seen the havoc wrought and the benefits that can be obtained by nuclear fission. The basis of materialism has been split altogether; the indissoluble atom has been dissolved. Scientists accept that matter is not solid, and that reality is to be found in the invisible.

Concurrent with that change in the climate of opinion you have the development and promotion of spiritual healing which, when it succeeds, demonstrates a power that is superior to matter.

Physical rest

WHEN you lack rest, the body pays the price. Sometimes the price is exacted that you must take to your beds for a complete rest. We cannot preach personal responsibility and tell you that there are exceptions to the operation of this law. Do not try to do too much. The body is only a machine and it must not be over taxed beyond its capacity.

Plane crashes, etc

THOSE who have knowledge of spiritual realities will not be affected. Those who have not will be affected because of the shock. But in the process of time, awareness and realisation will come.

Plants

Q Have flowers and plants consciousness?

NOT as you understand it, but they have response to vibrations which your world does not yet understand. There are many who can use these vibrations and succeed with flowers and vegetables and plants because they have sometimes by accident found the secret of those vibrations.

Positive thinking

Q By using this is it possible to have anything?

I THINK the question would have to be qualified because you cannot have anything that you want. There is a limit imposed by natural law on what you can attain. Were there not this limitation, then man could destroy and oppose the whole principle on which his world and the universe are founded. I am not opposing the idea behind positive thinking, but it would be absurd to say you can have anything you want. Suppose you desire the sun, you could not get it.

Population

Q Where do all these souls come from? We are told not to produce too many children. But if mankind goes on producing them they would be born.

IT may be the wrong word to use, but your question is based on a misconception. You do not create souls in your world. What you do is to create channels for souls to manifest. Spirit, the primal essence, is infinite, and infinity cannot be measured. What you do is to provide a means whereby spirit can incarnate and become individualised.

As spirit you have always existed. As individual spirit you started from the moment of conception. There are others who existed in your world before and who have a task to perform, redress to make, or something to achieve. They wait until they find the right vessels who will provide them with the opportunities for what they have to do.

Predetermination, and stellar control

WHAT is true is that the whole of life is a series of vibrations, radiations and emanations, and that you are influenced by every part of the natural order or being. All these cause some influence on you, but none of them is so potent that it exercises a power that you cannot alter.

It is not true that your life is predestined because at the moment of physical birth some star was in the ascendant. All planets, all nature, everything in the universe, all beings have some effect on you. But you are the master of your soul; you have personal responsibility, and you fix your own destiny according to your spiritual progress. That is how I see it.

Prejudice

PREJUDICE must be broken down, error must be fought. Truth will advance, however slowly and painfully, because it is truth. That which is worth having is worth achieving. Achievement comes through struggle. The prize is to him who dares and conquers, not to those who fear and are tempted to shirk their difficulties. Life is a school. Through hardship and struggle, striving and difficulty, adverse circumstance, storms and tempests, the spirit finds itself.

Privacy

Q Is there privacy of thought in the spirit world?

NO, you cannot conceal anything in our world, for all is known. In that, there is nothing of which to be ashamed. In your world you can cheat, lie and deceive. You can change your name legally if you like, but you cannot change your individuality.

Problems

PROBLEMS you will always have. They are there because in solving them you grow. If there were no problems you would cease to be alive in any sense of the word. The soul comes into its own not in the sunshine but in the storm.

Propaganda

Q *If the spirit world is interested in propaganda for Spiritualism why has it not made greater effort in regard to newspaper inquiries?*

OH, how little you know. It is always good that knowledge is spread. Who are you to judge the value of propaganda? You do not always know when souls are touched. We have our own methods. Our plans are all prepared, we only need the co-operation of your world to help us. But you must always remember we do not wave a wand. We offer no magical formulae. We seek to reveal the natural laws of the universe. We seek to touch the souls of your people so that they can understand that they are all parts of the Great Spirit and the laws of the Great Spirit can work through them. Our propaganda never ceases. It is not always done by the noises of your world, but by impressing the soul and the heart, by closer union with the spirit.

Prophetic dreams

Are they "transmitted" to the recipient from your side?

SOMETIMES they are. Sometimes they are prompted by their own loved ones who try to warn them. At other times, it is the experience of the spirit body itself which, freed from the limitations of earth, is able to glean something of the future and to bring back in the form of a dream a warning of what it has seen ahead in the path of time.

Protection of the body during sleep

Q *If our spirits leave our physical bodies during sleep and the body is left, as it were, untenanted, what is there to prevent some wandering earthbound spirit from possessing, or obsessing it? Is any spirit guide "on duty" to guard it against mal-occupation?*

WHAT prevents this happening is the natural law that you cannot be obsessed by undeveloped spirits unless you are in a condition to be obsessed. The spirit is not in the body, for the spirit does not belong to the same rate of vibration as the body. You – the real you – are not inside the body. You are not tucked in between your heart and lungs. You are consciousness expressing itself through the earthly machinery of your physical body.

All that happens when you sleep is that the consciousness, instead of expressing itself through the physical body, expresses itself through the spirit body and, because of that, it is expressing itself in the planes of spirit. There is no question of another coming in. It is not as if you have opened the door of your body and someone walks into the body and shuts the door. It is not like that at all. It is that the consciousness, still in charge of the body, expresses itself on another plane and returns as soon as it is time for it once more to associate itself with the physical body.

Psychic phenomena

Q *In the production of psychic phenomena, do you make use of materials in the room as well as the psychic powers of the sitters?*

YES, we make use of the carpet, the curtains, the books, even of the furniture. We who are not encased in matter have to use matter, and we obtain it to some extent from the actual substances that are here. We take a little from everything so as not to destroy things.

Psychic excellence

Q *Is it necessary to live a spiritual life in order to become a good psychic?*

THE better the life you live, the greater the instrument you become for the Great Spirit, for the higher your life, the more the Great Spirit within you is expressing itself. Your soul as it unfolds through the expression of the life which you live, makes you a greater instrument always.

Psychic gifts wrongly used

THE Great Spirit created you, not as puppets or marionettes. You were given a measure of free will, a choice. But it is restricted and limited. You cannot behave contrary to the natural laws.

If you have psychic gifts you can abuse them. That is your responsibility. You cannot have knowledge without the responsibility to which that knowledge is put.

Racial division

Q *How can we young people best channel our efforts towards healing the rift between coloured and white people?*

ONLY by example. If you show by your own lives that to you there are no yellow, red or black souls, that bodily skin has no relationship to soul qualities, then you will attract towards you those who are subjected to these bars, bans and barriers. The Great Spirit, with infinite wisdom, devised it that all His children should possess many coloured hues, so that together the perfect family make the rainbow. A white skin is no evidence of supremacy of spirit, neither is a coloured skin evidence of an inferior spirit. The real test is when you exhibit qualities of divinity, that is when the spirit is supreme.

Inter-racial superiority

I am a coloured man. Need I say more? Surely your world must be in error when it thinks that superiority can be determined by pigmentation, by the colour of the skin. Superiority is attained only through service. There is no other road. You are not greater or lesser in spirit if your skin is white, brown, red or black. The colour of your skin does not reflect the development of your soul. Your world tries to judge eternal problems by physical standards, but there is only one eternal standard – that is the standard of the spirit.

Racial inter-marriage

ALL races and all colours are part of the Great Spirit of all life who provides harmony in the perfect mixture of all hues. Look at nature's handiwork and realise that no matter how profuse or variegated are the colours of flowers in a vast garden, never is the note of disharmony or colour discord struck anywhere. When the colours are blended among men, you will be emerging towards the perfect race.

Responsibility for actions of others

YOU are not responsible for what others do or say. You are responsible only for what you do or say. Do not concern yourself with the opinions or actions of others.

Relationship between spirit and matter

YOU must not divorce matter from spirit and suggest that these are water-tight compartments that are in no way related. They are inter-related. While you are on the earth, spirit controls matter, but matter regulates the extent of spirit control. You cannot isolate matter from spirit.

Responsibility

Q *Are people responsible for all their own thoughts?*

PEOPLE regarded as normal are responsible for their own actions and that is the acid test. It is what they do that is of supreme importance.

Q *Does the spirit world agree with sanctions?*

YOU know my views. Life belongs to the Great Spirit, not to his children. They must not shorten life. This is against the law. And, if they do that, they must pay the price.

Q *But in this case the motive would be good, for it would be an attempt to stop the war.*

IF you sow the seeds of might, then out of those seeds can only come more might. Have you not been told before by those who are your earthly counsellors that it was a war to end war?

Seances and laughter

Q *Do you think laughter at seances is beneficial to results?*

THE happier you are in your soul, the nearer you are to the Great Spirit. Remember you are the Great Spirit and nothing in your world of matter can touch you. I have sought to teach you that for a long time. As long as you are worried by the things of matter, you will not learn the lesson.

I do not say disregard the things of matter, because you express yourself in the material world, and you have responsibilities to that world. But do not forget you are the Great Spirit and the Great Spirit is you. The power which belongs to the Great Spirit, which belongs to you, can raise you triumphant over all matter.

It is a power which, properly understood, can enable you to resist all evil, to overcome all sickness and to fight every obstacle. But few of you use it. You were taught about it many years ago by the Nazarene who said "The kingdom of heaven is within".

Religion – definition of

RELIGION is to serve the Great Spirit by serving his children. Religion has little to do with the conventional ideas of your world. Religion is that which enables the Great Spirit in you to be revealed in your life. Religion is that which increases the tie between you and the Great Spirit and between you and His other children. Religion is that which makes you go out into your world and give service wherever you can. Religion is service and service is religion.

All else does not matter. When the physical body falls away all the creeds over which for so long human beings have fought and strives are shown to be empty and vain, meaningless and purposeless, for they have not aided the growth of the soul by one iota. The growth of the soul is only increased by service, for as you forget self in the service of others so your own soul grows in stature and strength.

There have been, for too long, too many so-called religions, each with a variation of a message. The things which they hold most dear are in reality of no value. The things for which they have, in the past, caused blood to flow, tortured, maimed and burned, do not increase the spirit of man by one inch. They have divided mankind into opposite camps; they have created barriers; they have caused disputes; they have done everything that stands for disruption and disharmony. They have failed to unite the children of the Great Spirit. That is why we care not for buildings and conventional religion. We are not concerned with what a man calls himself. It is what he does that matters.

Religious education for children

TRUE education should consist in the dissemination of that knowledge which will enable children to be citizens of the world in which they live. It should instruct them in all the natural laws of the universe. It should make them aware of all the faculties with which they have been endowed, so that an unfolding of them will be of the greatest service to their own lives and to the world in which they live.

And so I come to the question of religion which, seeking to give guidance to the soul so that it can be prepared to face and to conquer all life's battles, obviously plays a paramount part in education. Because every child is part of the Great Spirit, because it is in essence a spiritual being, it is intended to live with all the benefits that freedom brings. If you cramp, if you restrict the soul of a child at an early age, you are denying it its elementary rights of freedom; you are condemning it to serfdom; you are making it a spiritual slave.

Freedom is the essence of all education. As I see it, the child will grow in freedom if it is taught the truths about religion. If those who teach give instructions based on a desire, not to give the child freedom but to teach it loyalty to ancient myth and fable, then they are poisoning the springs of the child's mind. No service is rendered to religion, to education or to the child by teaching it discarded creeds which, if it is intelligent, it will reject at the earliest possible age.

Then there will be inevitable reaction. It will turn its back on all those whom it considered misled it at a time when it had no means of resisting them. The young sapling is intended to grow straight as a tree, but if you give it nurture which is false, than you are helping to tamper with the very roots of its being and the growth will become stunted.

Bible quotes

Q *What did the Nazarene mean when he said, "Cast not your pearls before swine"?*

WHAT he had in mind was that you should not attempt to force great truth on unready souls.

Reincarnation

Q *Could you tell us anything about reincarnation?*

I HAVE the same difficulty as many of you experience. While I accept it, my instrument does not. If I have not succeeded in convincing him, I will not succeed in convincing others.

Q *You could tell us if it is the truth or not.*

FOR those who know, it is a truth; for those who do not know, it is not a truth.

Q *Is reincarnation true?*

THIS is a very vexed question because always there are differences of opinion in our world amongst those who know, and those who do not know. There are those who are just as emphatic in rejecting the idea of reincarnation as there are those equally emphatic in favouring it because of their experience. I am among the last category because it is something I have experienced. But as always, it is a confusing question because as you have heard me say so many times, it is not the same facet of the individuality that reincarnates.

It is done by those who have specific missions to perform, a voluntary act in order to redeem a pledge.

What incarnates is another aspect of the same individuality, and I do not mean personality. If you visualise man as an individual, who in his earthly life is like an iceberg in which you have one small portion manifesting and the larger portion not manifesting, then that is the end of one incarnation. In a successive incarnation, a portion of the submerged self will come into the world of matter – two different personalities, but one individual. And in the spirit life, as progression takes place, it is part of the submerged self that comes to the surface all the time.

Q *Why is there such a divided opinion among spirit guides and Spiritualists?*

BECAUSE some know and some don't. It is a question of experience. It takes a long time, as you count it, for this fact to be appreciated. People can be in our world for what you call ages and still be unaware of this truth. You must realise that the world of spirit is graded. It is not one of plane surface so to speak, where all have an equal level of attainment.

It is graded in spiritual development. You will find that the higher the ascent in the spiritual scale, the more recognition is there that there is reincarnation, because it happens but not in the facile form that is so often propounded.

Q *Is there an organisation in the spirit world to control reincarnation, to prevent mistakes being made?*

ALL these matters are simply resolved by the operation of natural law. You decide if you should incarnate. You do so at a time when you have a greater awareness and realise what can be achieved by becoming embodied in the earthly world. It does not require any group or organisation of beings. This is a matter the soul decides for itself.

Q *If there is karma, is there reincarnation?*

THERE is reincarnation, but not in the sense in which it is generally expounded. There is in our world a spiritual diamond which has many facets. These come into your world to gain experience and to add their quota to the diamond's lustre and brilliance. Thus the personalities that are incarnated are facets of the one individuality. There is no problem really. People get confused and say, "I was so-and-so last time and I will be somebody else next time." That doesn't matter. It is the facet which has its quota to contribute to the entirety of the diamond – in that sense there is reincarnation. What you express on earth is but an infinitesimal fraction of the individuality to which you belong. Thus there are what you call "group souls", a single unity with facets which have spiritual relationships that incarnate at different times, at different places, for the purpose of equipping the larger soul for its work.

Q *Will there always be another chance for everybody?*

OF course. If there were not a second chance, then the universe would not be ruled by divine love and justice. If the story of man ended with the earthly grave, then the world would be full of mistakes, full of people who had never had compensation or even retribution for the life they have lived.

The great glory of the knowledge we strive to bring to your world is that life does not end with death, that all who have suffered, that all who have failed, are provided with an opportunity of self-redemption, that the tears of frustration are wiped away in the knowledge of what can be achieved, that all who have desired to enrich their world and failed can add their lustre to mankind's growth.

Life goes on, and in doing so it provides everybody with another chance to express their innate gifts, the gifts that were denied a manifestation on earth; and conversely it provides the means of remedial discipline for those who have foolishly strutted and imagined that they had been able to escape the natural laws that ruled over all.

In that knowledge, the kindly and the decent have nothing to fear, it is only those who have been selfish who need be afraid.

Forgiveness

 Is there forgiveness in the spirit world?

THERE is forgiveness in your world and my world, but forgiveness does not expiate wrongdoing. When a person who has committed a wrong reaches the stage of asking for forgiveness, it means that realisation has dawned. But if he asks for forgiveness and forgiveness is accorded him, that does not mean that the act of wrong that was committed has been expunged. It is purely cause and effect. The act cannot be expunged until that which was wrong is put right.

Sceptics

 In discussion on reincarnation sceptics ask how those with Downs syndrome and the mentally deficient can possibly learn any lessons from earthly life?

THERE is no answer to the sceptics. The sceptic must find out for himself until he is satisfied. Then the scepticism will vanish. We are not theologians. This is not a matter of argument or a discussion in which you score points. This is a spiritual process in which awareness has to come to individuals.

As they achieve awareness they will understand some of the mysteries of life. They will not understand them all because if you could do so you would not be on earth. Earth is your school where you learn your lessons. Gradually as you learn them, and the knowledge comes, so your awareness grows. With it comes your ability to receive and understand more.

That is what the whole purpose of life is about. It is not for me to argue, to be challenged to debate. I can only enunciate certain fundamental truths which have endured and will endure. If they cannot be accepted, I am sorry. There is nothing I can do about it.

Progression

 Is each incarnation progressive or is it possible to end further down the ladder than when one started?

ALL life, especially that of the spirit, is progressive. I am referring specifically to the spirit because it is the one that really matters. Once you have knowledge, wherever it was gained, then as you apply it automatically you will grow spiritually and advance. And advance is always progression, though it will take eternity to achieve perfection.

Seance preparations

Q *Are any preparations made on the other side before a seance takes place?*

YES. Always we have to make the way clear. We have to harmonize our circles with yours. We have to prepare the way. We have to mix all the elements to get the best results. We work in highly organised bands for that purpose.

Q *Do precautions have to be taken before the seance is held, to exclude entities who operate forces that defeat the work?*

YES. The great precaution is to have love in your hearts and in your souls. Then only those who are filled with love can come near you.

Seeking evidence and spiritual growth

Q *We are told that the extent of our knowledge in spiritual matters is governed by our capacity to receive. Is it wise, therefore, for people who are spiritually unprepared to seek evidence through mediums?*

EVIDENCE has nothing to do with the growth of the soul. You ability to receive according to your capacity means how far can you reach out to the plane of spirit to receive truth? How far has your soul evolved so that it can understand truth? That must not be confused with the search for evidence. They do not go hand in hand. There are some that have evidence that life is continuous, but whose souls have not yet been touched by the spirit.

Second Coming

YOUR world has had prophecies of disasters for a long time. Often dates have been given when your world would be destroyed. There is no second coming. The Nazarene accomplished his earthly mission two thousand years ago. He continues his mission in the larger life which I inhabit. His is the guiding influence that directs our activities.

Service

WE are all channels of the Great Spirit. It is a privilege to serve. There is no religion higher than service. Service is the true coin of the spirit. It is noble to serve. To serve is to enrich the lives of others and your own. To serve is to bring comfort to those who think there is nothing left for them in your world.

It is in service that we find inner peace, tranquillity and repose. It is in service that we obtain steadfastness that enables us to have complete confidence in the overruling power, to strive to get closer and closer to the Great Spirit.

Service of the spirit

Q *Is it true that if you are a servant of the spirit, you must not expect a life of ease.*

ALL those who have work to do and are treading the spiritual path must find it not an easy path to follow. If spiritual mastery could be easily attained it would not be worth having. The prizes of the spirit have to be earned by arduous labour, but once gained they can never be lost.

Q *Why do certain people who attempt to give service in Spiritualism meet so much frustration in material affairs?*

BECAUSE he who would strive to serve must be tried and tested to the uttermost. Those who are to be soldiers in the army of the spirit must be strong enough to withstand any difficulty, to meet any obstacle and to rise triumphant over all troubles that assail them. What is the use of instruments of the spirit who will fall by the wayside when the first difficulty comes their way? Those who are to give the greatest service must be tried and tested in the purifying flames, for what emerges has the strength and durability of steel. All that which seems frustration is inevitably part of the plan of discipleship. If those who are called upon to serve had a life that was a bed of roses, with no trials, no stresses, no storms, no troubles, then their character might not emerge as it should and they might not be great enough to perform the task that awaits them.

Q *What is the soul?*

THE soul is the divine garment that every human wears. The soul is the light which the Great Spirit has given to every one of his children. The soul is the divine breath which enables the individual to function in the universe. The soul is the vital spark, the dynamic wellspring of his existence, that which relates him to the Great Spirit, that which makes him part of the infinity which broods over every manifestation of life. The soul is the imperishable garment that he will wear for all time. He is the soul, for the soul is the individual, the one part that reflects, thinks, decides, judges, weighs, loves, and that has every aspect of consciousness.

Souls old and new

Q *Where does the new spirit come from? Who decides into which conditions it will incarnate?*

THE essential difference between an old and a new soul is one of age. Obviously the old is older than the new. "Where does a new soul come from?" This question is very loosely phrased. Souls do not come from anywhere. Spirit has always been in existence. Spirit will always be in existence. It is the primal essence, the life force, the divine. It says in your Bible that "God is spirit".

If the questioner means, "Where does the individual soul come from?" then I say that at the moment of conception a particle of spirit incarnates to begin to express individuality on earth.

Q Do souls begin when men are conceived, or do they pre-exist?

I SAY there is pre-existence.

Q If we all belong to group souls then do we enjoy the experiences of others and also suffer the consequences?

YES, it is a wise experience because we all realise that we can contribute to the whole.

Q Has the soul evolved?

NO, the body has evolved. The soul is part of the Great Spirit which always was and always will be.

The soul has always been. It is individualised when it becomes incarnated into the human frame. The soul has no beginning and no end. It says in the Bible, "Before Abraham was I am." The spirit has always existed; the spirit was not created out of nothing.

Spirit is life. Life is universal. Souls, like spirits, do not have beginnings and ends. Spirit individualises when it incarnates into human form but as spirit it has always existed.

Spirit

Q At what times does the spirit enter the body?

AS a spirit you have always existed, because spirit is part of life and life is part of spirit. You have always existed.

Because you are part of the Great Spirit, you have never had a beginning, but you as an individual, as a separate, conscious individuality, must begin somewhere even in the stream of life. When conception takes place, the cells of the male and female meet and provide a vehicle for a particle of the life force to begin to express itself through a physical body. The life force is unexpressed until there is a vehicle through which it can manifest. That is what the earth parents provide. From the time the cells have coalesced and formed their union, the tiny particle of spirit has naturally attached itself and begins its expression in your world of matter. And I hold that this is the dawn of consciousness. From that moment it begins its conscious individual life. Thereafter it will always be an individual entity of its own.

Q When does it take up residence in the physical body?

I HAVE been asked this question many times. I have always given the same answer. When there is conception there is life. And where there is life there is spirit.

Sin

Q *Is it possible to sin the world of spirit?*

OF course it is possible to sin in our world. The sins of the spirit world are the sins of selfishness, but in our world they are speedily revealed. They are known as soon as the thought is in the mind, and the effect is seen much more quickly than it is in your world of matter. It registers on the one who commits the sin and makes him spiritually lower than he was before. It is difficult to define more clearly in your language what these sins are, except that they are sins of selfishness.

Sleep experiences

Q *Do they help us when we pass on?*

YES, nothing is wasted. The law is perfect. Those of us who have lived for many years marvel at the perfection of the law, and when we hear the puny minds of your world criticise the Great Spirit – how little they know! The less they know the more they express themselves.

Sleep state

Q *Are many people engaged in working in their sleep state, or are the visits to the spirit world used solely for preparation for the larger life?*

SOME of you do work, because there are many that you can help in your sleep state. But usually it is a preparation. You are taken to those places which will help you to be ready for your work when you leave the world of matter. If that were not done, the shock of coming from one sphere of expression to another would be so great that it would take you a long time to recover.

That is why it is easier for those who have knowledge when they come to our world. Others have to sleep and rest for a long time, until they can adjust themselves. If you have knowledge, then you pass from one state to another and you are aware of the new life. After all, it is just like opening a door and coming into the sunshine. You must get accustomed to the light.

Q Do we remember sleep experiences?

WHEN your spirit is released from its body, you are freed from your brain, which is your limitation in the world of matter. The consciousness now has experiences on our vibrations, according to your grade of evolution, and it is conscious of its experiences whilst it has them. But, when you go back to your body of matter and try to capture the experiences of the spirit, you cannot do so because one is greater than the other. The smaller cannot hold the greater and you get distortion.

It is as if you had a little bag and tried to get lots of things into it. You could only get some of the things into the bag, and the more you pushed the more out of shape they would become. That is what happens to you when you return to your bodies.

But if your soul is already evolved and you have reached an advanced stage of consciousness, then you are aware of the spirit realms. Then you can quite easily train the brain to remember.

Solitude

 Q Do you believe good is achieved by mystics who cut themselves off from the world and meditate in solitude?

THAT all depends what is meant by "good". It may be that withdrawing from the world of matter can help to unfold the powers of the spirit. To that extent it is good. Yet to me it is greater to be in the world yet not of the world, serving the world by the powers that the Great Spirit has given you, after you have unfolded them yourselves through striving, through effort, through development.

 Is it true that by solitude good can only be done to oneself?

THE greatest good is when you forget yourself in the service of others. It is not wrong to develop your powers. It is better to develop them so that when they are developed they can be used in the service of the children of the Great Spirit.

Speakers

Q Should speakers concentrate more an attacking what is wrong (racialism, nationalism, cruelty to animals and children)?

YES, as long as you stress that the reason why you attack these cruelties, misunderstandings and discriminations is because they are spiritually wrong apart from being physically wrong. You have a unique attitude towards these problems because you are aware of spiritual realities.

Because man is a spirit he must have a body fit enough to be its temple. Therefore his mind must have the education that is essential to equip that temple. His body must have the right conditions, the right home, the right clothing, the right food, because it is spiritually necessary for this to be so. It is spiritually wrong to be cruel to animals. It is spiritually wrong to have race or colour discrimination. The soul has no colour. It is not yellow, red, black or white. If you stress the spiritual aspect, then you are emphasising the most important contribution you can make.

Spirit bodies

Q When we pass out of the physical body, is the one we use in the spirit world as real and solid as the one we leave behind?

FAR more real and far more solid than the one you leave behind in the world of matter, for your world is not the real world at all. It is only the shadow cast by the world of spirit. Ours is the reality and you will not understand reality until you pass into the world of spirit.

Spiritual development

Q You have said, "In all the troubles and perplexities of life people need have no fears, as we can find a solution for every problem within our own selves." How can we achieve this?

YOU must remember that the whole of humanity is not at exactly the same level of consciousness. There are thousands of groups all at different stages of progress. If you had reached that stage of mental and spiritual unfoldment where you could allow your inner qualities to be expressed; if you had arrived at that stage of your development where you knew how to be still, how to turn within to find in your latent divinity all that you re- quired, you would have the answer to your question. The fact that you ask "how" means that there is still development to be achieved. You are part of the Great Spirit. That spirit is within you. That portion which you possess has within it, potentially, all the perfection that belongs to the Great Spirit of all life. If you can harmonise yourself with it; if you can learn how to still yourself and hold yourself in perfect poise, when no wavering doubts or thoughts can come near you because you are at one with yourself and, therefore, at peace with the Great Spirit, then fear cannot touch you, for your soul would be beyond such vibrations.

I do not say it is easy. I say it can be done, and there are many thousands who have abolished fear from their beings.

Q *I am not happy about what you said on equal opportunities. While the spiritual essence in a soul may be the same, the instruments through which that essence will be expressed are not of equal efficiency. We cannot all gain benefit through equal opportunities. Either the opportunities presented to us vary according to our talents, or the opportunities are equal, but we are not fairly endowed so that we all have a reasonable chance of making use of them.*

NO, I'm sorry I cannot agree. Every human being who incarnates into the world of matter has a seed of divinity, otherwise he could not incarnate. Life is spirit and spirit is life. You have the seed of the spirit which is intended to flower. Its flowering depends upon the conditions it receives and which will affect its growth. There are equal opportunities for all human beings to develop their spiritual natures. I did not say they would attain equality of spiritual status. I said the opportunities were there. It does not matter if you are rich or poor, the service you give is not dependent upon the physical knowledge that you have.

Spiritual gifts

IF you are endowed with any gift, no matter what its form, you should develop it so that others can be served and enlightened.

Q *What is the different between psychic and spiritual or are they the same?*

ALMOST the same, but not quite. You can have all the psychic faculties, but they do not become spiritual faculties until they are used for a spiritual purpose in association with spiritual people in our world. You all have the faculties of the psychic body but it is not until these faculties are developed and blended with the power of the spirit that they become spiritual gifts.

Spiritual growth

THE spirit grows through kindness, tolerance, sympathy, love, service and the doing of good works. Character evolves only when you allow the divine spirit to be made manifest in your daily lives. If you harbour unkind thoughts, thoughts of hatred or malice, of vengeance, of selfishness, you yourself will be the victim and you yourself must pay the price in a warped, distorted and thwarted character.

Spiritual institutions

Q *Why is it that in our spiritual institutions there are so many business and material considerations which require people who are capable in these fields to deal with all the problems and very often this is done to the detriment of the spiritual teaching?*

DO you know your Bible? Let me quote some familiar words to you. "Seek ye first the kingdom of God, and his righteousness, and all these things shall be added unto you". What do you think that means?

Q *I would say you have to look for the spiritual side first.*

SPIRIT is king, matter is servant. Spirit comes before matter. When the spirit is right matter will be right. It is all a question of priorities. No worthwhile cause will suffer for want of money.

Spirit errors

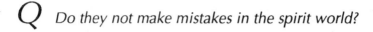

Q Do they not make mistakes in the spirit world?

YES. The astral planes are very much like your world. People who live there are very much at a similar stage of development to the average person in your world. They are neither angels nor demons. They are just ordinary people, not too high nor too low. They make mistakes due to faulty judgments, lack of wisdom. Mistakes due to rancour, to hatred and selfishness: the mistakes that come from imperfection.

Spiritual pathway

IT would be folly to tell any disciple who seeks greater truth and understanding that the path will be an easy one. Spiritual mastery is slowly attained. The prizes of the spirit are not quickly earned. But once they are in your possession they are there for all time. They will never be lost, which is something that can never be said for your material possessions.

Spiritual progress

Q What is the greatest aid in spiritual progress, love or knowledge?

I WOULD say on balance that it is love, if I am allowed to define love as the love that embraces not only one individual but all humanity. If you have reached that stage where you feel that you can have love for all, not only for those whom you like or who are near and close and dear to you, then that is an indication that your feet are very firmly planted on the road of spiritual progress and it shows that you do have knowledge of spiritual principles. So that love, I think, is the greater aid, because you can have knowledge without love, but you cannot have love without knowledge.

Spiritualist Movement

Q We must be honest and say that the Spiritualist movement and mediumship in general are at a very low level.

STOP there. We are not concerned with what you call the Spiritualist movement. We are concerned with individuals who are prepared to develop the gifts of the spirit, whether within or without organisations is not very important. Organisations should perform or fulfil certain purposes. It is for the organisers to concern themselves with that problem.

Our responsibility is always to help any individual who desires to serve wherever he can. Names do not bother me. Spiritualist, Theosophist, Rosicrucian, these are only labels. What matters is that each should seek the truth according to his capacity. Mediumship is important because it means that there is a person on whom has been conferred a gift which can be used to give one of the greatest services in your world. It is a tremendous responsibility and imposes, or should do, a sacred trust on its owner.

Realms of spirit

Q If the spirit world is a replica of this one, are all the ugly things duplicated – slums, bad working conditions and so on?

THESE conditions are duplicated in the lower realms of the astral world because they are the natural environment for many who cannot picture life existing under any other circumstances. You must remember that this is not the reality, but rather the expression of the mentality of those who dwell on such a plane of living. The moment they realise they are not compelled to live in squalor and dirt – in conditions that proximate to the worst of the earth life – then they are freed; and the only ones who dwell there are those who are first of all so ignorant that they cannot conceive of anything different, and those who are not yet spiritually ready to move upwards. You must realise that it is all part of the wise provision that there should be easy steps in the unfoldment of the spiritual life. If there were no easy steps, then the shock caused by the transition could be a very, very terrible thing.

Trends of Spiritualism

Q What is your view of present trends in Spiritualism?

THE tide ebbs and flows. There are periods of activity and there are periods of stillness. You cannot maintain any movement by one outburst of energy. On the surface it would seem that so much progress has been made, that tremendous victories have been gained, but, against that, there are millions of people who are completely ignorant of the truths of spirit. As I have always told you, what you call Spiritualism is only a name. To me, it is the natural law in operation. I am concerned with the spreading of knowledge so that ignorance may be vanquished. I applaud any effort by the individual or a group, to spread that knowledge.

From what has been revealed to me, I know that the overall plan must succeed. Spirit truth has come to stay in your world. It may be that there are occasional ebbs. It may be that there are periods of enthusiasm and, at other times, indifference. It may be that some grow weary in the task. But this is only a very small part of a large picture. The emphasis in your world is on healing. That is deliberate, not accidental. It is making its mark in a manner that is not accidental. It is making its mark in a manner that is designed to awaken the consciousness of those who very largely should be bound to realise that spirit power is the reason for their cures, their improvements, their amelioration.

I am never pessimistic with regard to the truths of the spirit. I am always optimistic, because I know the power which is behind us. I rest content in what I have seen. I know that people in your world can hinder, retard or delay, but they cannot stop the advance of spirit truths. That is all that matters. It is part of a tremendous plan. It does not matter what the clergyman says, what the doctor says, or what the scientist says. They have no power to prevent spirit truths from being made known more and more as time goes on in your world.

Contribution of Spiritualism

Q What is the greatest contribution Spiritualism has to make to the modern world?

THE greatest contribution that this knowledge has is to bring freedom in all its diverse ramifications to the children of the Great Spirit. It frees them from all the bondage to which they have been subject. It removes them from the prison-house of ignorance by showing them that the door of knowledge has opened wide for them. It enables them to live in the sunlight instead of in the shadow. Man was born to be free to dwell in liberty; he was not born to be a slave, bound and fettered. His life should be full of richness, the richness of mind and body and spirit. All knowledge should be open to him, all truth, all wisdom, all inspiration. He should dwell in the splendour of the spirit with none of the cramping, irksome, vexatious restrictions imposed upon him by those who would deny his heritage and thwart his destiny.

Faith v Spiritualism

 Is it better that Spiritualism should grow as it is growing as an influence, rather than as a formally organised faith?

I WOULD deny that it is a faith. It is a knowledge. You cannot control the breath of the wind; you cannot control the growth or the spread of knowledge. Truth will blossom of her own accord. You cannot regulate it. You can only provide the means by which it becomes accessible to more and more people. What the effect of this knowledge will be you cannot estimate before; you cannot lay down any rules or control the channels of its dissemination. All you can do is to be faithful to your own responsibility, to discharge your duty in the light of your understanding, to help where you can, to pass on what you have received, and let the balm of the spirit take its own course. It is a leaven. It will continue to infiltrate and permeate throughout all branches of human activity. Each must do what he thinks best and spread knowledge according to the way he thinks it will be of service.

Unity in service

 We have a big problem inside our movement. We have not the necessary unity, which we should have, to be very powerful. It is our great concern to find a way to better this condition. Have you any comments on this?

YOU will not achieve this very easily. Unity cannot be ordered. It can be achieved only by gradual growth as understanding comes. One of the great difficulties is that the whole of mankind is at different levels of intellectual, moral and spiritual attainment. There is no one common standard. Even in your own movement you have many clashes based upon the simple fact that each is at a different stage of evolution. Spiritual realisation can come only with advancing spiritual attainment. What is so clearly patent, when you have established that unity with higher beings, is not something you can share with others who have not reached that stage. Therefore you must attempt to accomplish the greatest good with the means at your disposal.

This is not a problem which is unfamiliar to us, because we are confronted with it all the time. We have to work with earthly beings, some of whom do not measure up to the standard that we would like. And so we have to do the best we can. You will find gradually that light does spread. The important factor is that you organise gatherings, like you have had here, where people of different ideas and languages, from differing lands with different traditions and environments can meet and learn from one another. They see, for example, what others have achieved, so that where they are backward they receive the stimulus to advance. Do not worry. Do the best you can. When you can do no more, relax and let us take over. You are only asked to do the best you can, no more.

Q Could you perhaps point out a better way?

THERE is no better way that the truth. The problem of reincarnation, for example, is one of the difficulties you will not resolve. Here, again, it is not a question so much of trying to obtain conviction by what is called evidence – these are only words. Conviction comes from within. When the soul is ready it knows – that is the only conviction that matters. Science is constantly changing and enlarging its boundaries. Knowledge is not fixed, but conviction is the inner realisation that you at last have come face to face with truth.

You will not get agreement, not for a long time, if ever at all, in your world. To those who accept reincarnation, it is so simple and easy. And to those who do not, it seems so difficult. You must be patient and wait. It will not destroy your organisation. It is good that they will argue and that they will disagree. Nature abhors a vacuum. Inertia is contrary to the laws of nature. Action and reaction are both opposite and equal but part of the same power. You cannot stand still, you must argue and discuss. Out of the melting pot, out of the cauldron, when the seething and bubbling subsides, truth will gradually emerge.

Spiritual qualities

 Can you say how one can become more articulate in expressing feelings to help other people?

TRY occasionally to still yourself for a while, to withdraw from all the jangling discord of your world into the silence of your own soul. When you are quiet, passive, receptive, we can come very close to you, for your silence is our opportunity. If you are never still, you set up such a rush of vibrations that they bar the passage and make it almost impossible for us to get close to you.

Suffering

THERE is no suffering so strong that you do not possess the inner strength and can call upon an outer power to enable you to overcome it. The burden is never heavier than can be borne. If you strive to live in harmony with the natural laws you will find an inner peace, tranquillity and resolve that will ensure that you always come through.

Let me explain to you how the things of the spirit work. People in your world talk about the mystery of suffering, the purpose of illness, the reason for crises, difficulty and obstacles. These are the challenges that the human soul must encounter because they provide first the catharsis and then the catalyst that will enable them to appreciate spiritual truth. As low as any soul can sink so correspondingly can it rise. That is the law of polarity, the law which says that action and reaction are equal and opposite. Hate and love, light and dark, storm and peace, these are opposite sides of the same coin.

Q *Does Silver Birch agree that all suffering is brought on by ourselves, that this is the teaching of karma and implies reincarnation?*

ALL suffering is the result of cause and effect. There is no suffering which comes to any man, be hazard or chance or coincidence; it is due to circumstances in which he has involved himself. It is part of his own pilgrimage, whether in this earthly life or in another. I cannot prove that; I cannot demonstrate that; but, nevertheless, that is what I hold to be true.

Starting a home circle

Q *What advice can you give to one who wishes to start a home circle?*

YOU must tell him to have plenty of patience, to be prepared for constant sittings before the power of the spirit can express itself. He should choose a group who blend in harmony, where there is no mental friction, where all can unite with a common interest.

They should meet once a week at the same time, for an hour or perhaps a little longer, begin with prayer and then be passive. But each, beforehand, should search his own heart and ask the motive, the desire, what it is he hopes to achieve. If the motive be for service, then let them continue. If it be the desire to play with toys, that is not enough. But if they wish to come together in one place, all of one accord, to enable the spirit to reveal itself, then those who are physically in tune will be touched by that power and gradually it will reveal itself.

Our aim is not to please the sensation seeker who desires some new thrill for his jaded being, but to uplift mankind and to make it find once again those inherent powers almost lost through the lack of usage.

Suicide

 Is it ever permissible for a person to pass on by his own act, such as the one who is left of a devoted companionship?

NO, you must live your lives according to the Law, for the Law is always perfect in its operation. It is controlled by perfect love and by the Great Spirit who is in all things and who works through all things. You have no right to interfere with the operation of the Law, and if you do you must pay the price for cutting yourself off.

If you force the apple to drop from the tree before it is ripe, then the apple has no sweetness. If you force yourself to go into the next stage of life before your spirit is ready, then you will have to pay the price in the long adjustment that you will have to make. It will also have the effect of causing you to be separate from the ones you love, for you will have made a gulf.

What is the status of suicide in the spirit world?

YOU cannot answer that right away. It depends on the earthly life that has been lived; it depends upon the qualities that have been developed; it depends upon the soul's progress; and, above all these things, it depends on the motive. The churches are wrong when they say that all suicide comes in the same category; it does not. While you have no right to terminate your earthly existence, there are undoubtedly in many cases, ameliorating factors, mitigating circumstances, to be considered. No soul is better off because it has terminated its earthly existence. But it does not automatically follow that every suicide is consigned for aeons of time into the darkest of the dark spheres.

Does the suicide suffer any great setback when he takes his own life?

OF course. Although there are always exceptions, but they form the minority. As you know, in all cases I always say the motive is the dominating interest. But your soul is judged on its own conduct. You write with your own hand your own book of life. The entries are indelible; you cannot cheat. You judge yourselves. The law is fixed and unalterable. We say face up to your responsibility. No situation is as dark as you think it is.

Survival of the strongest

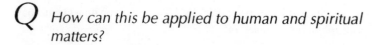

Q How can this be applied to human and spiritual matters?

HAVE you heard of symbiosis? Isn't that a law of nature? And isn't it a fundamental law that co-operation existing in nature enables nature to fulfil its purpose?

The tree absorbs the poisons in the atmosphere, purifies it, and enables you to be healthier. Is that strength, or is it not harmony and co-operation at work?

Q Isn't it a dangerous thing to impress the facts of Survival – such as the proximity and awareness of loved ones – on those who are young enough to remake their earthly lives after loss? Might not an expression of conviction and fact tie youth to those we call dead, with mental complications and feelings of disloyalty?

NO, life is always lived better when truth reigns supreme. Ignorance is as much an enemy as prejudice or superstition. Ignorance must be banished, for ignorance belongs to the darkness and you are meant to be children of light. When you have knowledge, you can adjust your life in the light of that knowledge; when you have darkness you have no principle or reason to guide you day by day. We have enthroned knowledge and reason as the guides for all human conduct. When you have knowledge and apply your reason, then you should be able to live your life in accordance with standards that will make your pilgrimage on earth worth while.

Survival of Mankind

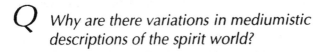 *Will man survive?*

YES, man will survive. There is a limitation placed by natural law on what man can do to the planet on which he lives. He cannot destroy the whole of the planet and all that it contains. Now this is part of man's free will; his choice as to whether he will rise to the divinity within him or whether he will fail. In that case he will not fulfil himself. He will pass to our world unequipped and unready and have to learn all over again.

No man, and no combination of men, have the power to thwart divine will. They can delay, they can harass and they can impede. Infinite wisdom and love rule the universe. These will prevail because that is the law.

Spirit world

Q Why are there variations in mediumistic descriptions of the spirit world?

YOU have to realise that we live in an infinite world and thus there must be an infinite variety of experiences for its dwellers. Life in our world is graded spiritually and thus there are differences of experience for all who are here.

Anyone communicating with you can transmit only what he or she has experienced at that time. With progress, that soul will move to another plane of being which can cause him or her to revise an opinion previously held.

So it depends on the evolution of the communicator as to what pictures are being transmitted to your world. You must remember that the closer the communicator is to your world, the more limited is the ability to express what is higher in the scale of spiritual values which he or she has yet to attain.

My advice is always the same. Treat every communication from our world with reason. If your commonsense says, "No, I cannot accept this," then reject it. We are not infallible. We have not attained perfection, because that requires eternity. The process, as I have already said, is infinite.

Q Is there only one spirit world?

YES, but it has an infinite number of expressions, and life on planets other than earth is embraced as well as your world of matter, because they have their spiritual expression as well as their physical.

Time

Q Is time artificial?

TIME is not artificial but it has many dimensions. What is artificial is your measurement of it. Time itself is a reality. It exists. Space exists. But your measurements are not accurate because you view time and space from a limited focus. When you have the knowledge of other factors, then the focus becomes more in line with the truth.

Thought

Q Are the thoughts we send to loved ones who have passed on always received?

IT is not possible to give a straightforward "Yes" or "No", because it depends upon the evolution of the soul. If the one who has passed into my world is on the same mental and spiritual plane as the one in your world, then he will receive the thoughts, but if the two are so far removed from one another that they are on different planes, then the one who has passed on will not receive the thoughts.

 Is there any truth is the doctrine that thought possesses real tangible power?

THOUGHT has its limitations in a material world where matter is the basis of recognition. It must be so, but, on the other hand, I do not wish to dismiss the value of thought, or the place that it has in the scheme of life.

Thuggery

 We have had the experience of young bullies and skinheads. Do you think it is necessary to be armed when we go out for a walk? There is no reason why we should allow them to knock us down for money. Should we fight back?

IT is never right that evil should be tolerated or violence encouraged. It has been said that those who live by the sword shall perish by the sword. It is your duty to protect your physical body, the only means by which the spirit can express itself on earth. You should use your reason in all matters appertaining to your earthly existence. We have no sympathy for violence, the spirit cannot work that way. The spirit expresses itself in tranquillity, calm and peace and quiet confidence. Violence is one of the by-products of the gospel of materialism. Try not to be engulfed by this gloom resulting from violence and terrorism. Try to rise above it, to be in the world but not of the world, to be aware of your spiritual nature, your divine potential, so that at least you become a little lighthouse of the spirit with rays that will help those seeking to find you.

Tolerance

TOLERANCE is the essence of spirituality. If there is bigotry, there is no spirituality.

Transition

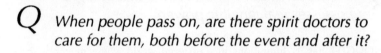

Q When people pass on, are there spirit doctors to care for them, both before the event and after it?

YES, because they have to help the spirit body to release itself and to be prepared, as much as is possible, for its greater life. That is why, frequently, before death takes place, the one who is making the transition becomes aware of loved ones who are gathered around, helping the soul to free itself.

Trials and tests in spiritual mastery

IN order to become ambassadors for the Great Spirit, the human channels have to be tried and tested so that their latent strength can rise to the surface. They are then ready to meet the challenges that their mission will inevitably make them encounter.

It is not possible to achieve even the first steps in spiritual mastery unless you are ready to do so by a process which means that you must suffer.

Suffering is the crucible. Those on whom the Great Spirit, with infinite wisdom, has bestowed the gift of healing must experience difficulty, sorrow, crises and trial so that they can have compassion for the ones who will come to them in their suffering and ask for healing.

Truth

Q *Is it only the minority who can understand spiritual truth?*

THE truths of the spirit are very simple. They can be grasped by all; they are intended for all. It is not part of the divine plan that there should be a small sect, a divinely favoured few. It is the many we are trying to reach because it is the many with whom we are concerned.

Q *Many young people seek truth. We want a better world in which to bring up our children. Why must man kill and maim his brother? Why must he hate those of a different race or creed? Why is there so little love in the world? We want peace on earth, but when and how will it come? How can we succeed where the older and so-called wiser have failed? We are young, strong and willing and wish to serve in the war against ignorance and stupidity, greed and hate. What then is your advice?*

THAT seems quite a question. Ignorance and stupidity, the words you use, have been in your world for a very long time. There is no magical formula that will abolish them overnight. Nature works by evolution, not revolution. All growth proceeds slowly and inexorably. Any attempt to force physical growth beyond its ordained limits inevitably results in disaster. Similarly, any attempt to accelerate spiritual growth must fail.

I say this in no spirit of pessimism. I know that all those that have been permitted to catch a glimpse of spiritual, divine reality must be optimistic. They realise that man, however foolish or reckless he may be, has imposed on him restrictions. He is subject to natural laws over which he has no control. There is no instant panacea that we have to offer. All we can say is that as knowledge spreads and ignorance, as a result, recedes, so the divisions between man and man become fewer, the wars will abate, the greed lessons and the areas of light increase. It is not within our power to transform the earthly scene.

All that we can do is to inculcate into those who are ready to receive knowledge the truths that will teach them how to order their lives aright. Man has, again within prescribed limits, a freedom of choice. He can share with the infinite power in the processes of creation and help in the forward march of evolution. He can hinder, he can delay, he can deter. This is his contribution. The Great Spirit, with infinite wisdom, did not create puppets, marionettes or automatons. Man was endowed with latent wisdom and with all the divine attributes that the Great Spirit, or God as you call it, possesses. So man must make his choice. He must learn that war solves no problems, but only creates fresh ones; that greed and selfishness contain within themselves the seeds of their own disasters. Many years ago the Nazarene said that he who takes to the sword shall perish by the sword. Man must learn these lessons by himself. All that you can individually do is to spread knowledge wherever you can. If you succeed in bringing light and truth to one in addition to yourself, then your earthly life will not have been in vain. This is the only answer I can give.

Unconsciousness

 Is there a difference between the state of unconsciousness caused by a brain injury, and unconsciousness in sleep?

OH, yes. When you are unconscious because of an injury that is something that interferes with the normal harmony between your spirit and your body. When you sleep, that is the normal thing, for the spirit knows that every night the vibrations of the physical body slow down and the spirit prepares itself by coming to our world. One is the normal part of your experience and the other is an abnormal happening that interferes with your make up. In one case the spirit leaves the body voluntarily, in the other it is forced out because the body is unfit for it to function through it.

Q Should we not support the United Nations?

IS there a desire among those who are counsellors of nations for peace? Is peace in their hearts and in their souls? Are they determined to abide by the eternal principles of the laws of the Great Spirit, or do they merely seek to stop that which might become a menace to their own countries? Do they not still think in terms of wealth and nation and race, instead of in the terms of the Great Spirit and His children? We deal with the eternal principles, with the Great Spirit and His laws and their operation. There is no other way.

You may succeed for a time with your half-measures, but out of evil there will always come evil. One day, your world will realise that love can overcome evil because love is the expression of the Great Spirit. When, in the spirit of love, all people seek to solve their problems, then peace will reign in your world. But all desires which are contrary to the law of love will always produce disruption, chaos and bankruptcy. You must strive to deal with roots, for by no other way can you have eternal peace.

Vegetarianism

Q Shall we, after we pass on, be punished for having eaten animal food?

WHEN you have reached that stage in your evolution when you know it is not right to eat the lesser creation of the Great Spirit, then you inflict on yourself a punishment for doing that which you know to be wrong. If you have not reached that stage of evolution, then your soul is not yet aware that it is wrong and there will be no punishment. Always there is a price to be paid for knowledge. That price is responsibility.

Would this be a happier world and would people become healthier if they were vegetarians?

I WILL answer the question by saying that in my view the answer must be "Yes". From many points of view meat eating is deleterious. These points of view include physical, mental and spiritual aspects. Not only is the moral question involved, the health question is involved too. From the spiritual point of view I would go so far as to contend that, with the evolution of the race, vegetarianism will become the increasing diet of larger numbers of people.

Vivisection

 Can vivisection be right when it is undertaken with a good motive?

NO. How can that which is cruel be right? How can that which causes pain, which inflicts torture, be right? It is contrary to all that we teach. It is wrong to experiment on those who are not capable of resisting.

War

THE Great Spirit, with infinite wisdom and love, has created earthly children and given them some free will. The Great Spirit has also arranged the whole of their minds, spirits and bodies so that they can unfold the divinity that lies within them which, in full flower, can provide infallible signposts as to how individuals should live. The Great Spirit could have created all the earthly children as marionettes, puppets, whose actions would be strictly regulated with no power of choice, no freedom. But you cannot have free will without, at the same time, the responsibilities of your actions. If you have the choice to do good, you also have the choice to do evil. Good and evil are opposite sides of the same coin. So are love and hate, light and dark, storm and peace. This is a polarity. Yours is the choice as to which it should be. So you must come back to the motive and ask: "Why do people wage war? What is it that they seek to share in common? Or is it to gain domination over others?" You must answer these questions. It is your world. You can make it a paradise or a hell because you have the means and the choice to do so.

Q *I cannot – a single person cannot – do that.*

YOUR world is made up of an aggregate of single units. The more single units are determined to abolish greed and rapacity and cruelty and despotism, the more they are likely to succeed as their numbers grow. Your responsibility is for your life, your actions, your words, your thoughts. Nobody will ask you to pay the price or to receive the reward for what others have done. That is the law. There will be for a long time, outbreaks of war somewhere because man has not learned a simple truth. All are part of one spiritual family. Though you may destroy bodies you cannot destroy spirits. We are not responsible for man's inhumanity to man. This is cause and effect in operation.

World strife

Q *Have you anything to say to people who are very concerned with the way much of the world is going: the materialism, the violence, the dreadful things that are on the increase in the so-called civilised parts of the world?*

I WOULD say that the will of the Great Spirit must prevail, that those who serve the cause concerned with the amelioration of man and other creatures, those who dedicate themselves to the task of alleviating suffering, ending cruelty, helping wherever they can, should never lose heart. The great purpose will be fulfilled in your world, slowly, gradually and sometimes painfully. You get these phases of violence, discord, clashes, war, brutality, because your world is in the melting pot. So many traditional ideas have been discarded. In the maelstrom it is hard for those in the thick of it to see the divine purpose fulfil itself. Do not be disheartened. The great and important fact is that the truths and the power of the spirit have effected lodgement in so many lands and cannot be driven out.

War criminals

Q *What will be the fate of war criminals in your world?*

THE natural law will take care of every individual, no matter who he may be. The law is perfect in its operation. Effect always follows cause with mathematical precision. No individual has the power to alter by one hair's breadth the sequence of cause and effect. That which is reaped must be that which is sown, and the soul of every individual registers indelibly all the results of earthly life. He who has sinned against the law bears on his own soul the results of his earthly action, and there will be no progress until reparation has been made for every sinful deed. There is no need to think that any man or woman or child can escape the results of earthly life. The whole stress of our teachings is to tell mankind that the universe is ruled by unchanging, immutable laws, and the Great Spirit cannot be mocked, cheated or deceived. You will have that heaven or hell which you have made by your own earthly life.

Q *Did not any good at all come out of the sacrifices of those who "died" in the War?*

I CAN see none. Your world of matter is nearer chaos today, and is more filled with destruction, than it was when your "Great War" began.

Can so much heroism be spent in vain? Is there no spiritual repercussion?

THERE is on the part of the individuals who made the sacrifice, because their motive was good. But do not forget that your world has betrayed them. It has made their sacrifice pointless, because it has continued in its materialism.

 Is there not some reason for war in the cosmos?

NO. You make wars in your world. We do not make them in ours. But whenever you have the lust to kill, you always attract those who are bound to earth with similar desires.

Youth

Q How would you suggest we can get the young ones interested in spirit truth?

I THINK the interest must be aroused not on the basis of trying to prove they can achieve communication with people in our world because, generally speaking, youth has not endured the experiences, the soul-searching, heart-breaking experiences of physically losing ones they love. I would say that the appeal must be to reason and to intelligence, to offer them spiritual truths which will appeal to their logical instincts, not to ask them to have faith, hope or belief, but to question everything we say on the ground of its being reasonable, satisfactory and showing that it has all the hallmark of truth.

Q *Would you recommend that they join a development circle?*

NOT at first. I would recommend they join groups for meditation which would appeal to them more, so as to give the inner faculties a chance of expression.

Q *Would not that rather make them join so-called mystics?*

IF they do they will have taken the wrong turning. That is the choice their free will must make. You must allow them to unfold in their own way. When they are ready they will receive. When the pupil is ready the master comes.

Youth v Society

Q *In speaking of the rebellion of the young against organised society, a questioner asked, "Do you agree that possibly they are much more attuned to the other world and are responding to guidance from it without knowing it?"*

I DON'T mind the revolt. It is the violence to which I object.

Q *The young are seeking a God based on love. Their ideas are based on love. They are not church-conscious but God-conscious. Is that right?*

IT is youth's function to revolt. If youth accedes it would cease to be youth. Youth must quest, search, rebel. You have had cataclysmic upheavals in your world which have changed convention and caused the loss of respect for established teaching. Do not blame the young because they seek to find what they think are better ways of governing the world in which they live.

 In dealing with the question of young people on LSD who were becoming possessed of harmful entities, the guide said:

UNFORTUNATELY some of these drugs open a psychic centre that can reach out no higher than the lowest astral field surrounding your earth. The beings who can invade them are like themselves, often drug addicts, or alcoholics seeking satisfaction because their unevolved state chains them. They are not free. The healing power is the catalyst. This can help to clarify the whole complex situation created by physical, spiritual and astral conditions getting mixed up.

Zodiac

 Does the star under which you were born affect personality?

I THINK all of these planets have radiations which affect the physical body, and things which affect the physical body have some effect on the spirit; but the spirit is supreme; the spirit is pre-eminent, and there is no star or planet or constellation or galaxy which can prevent you from mastering all the physical influences which affect your body. I mean that you are part of the Great Spirit, and because you are divine, because the power of creative life is within you, because you are a portion of that power which fashioned all life, you can rise triumphant over all that might hold your body in subjection. I am an influence on you, the people you meet are influences on you; the books you read are influences on you; but they are influences not overwhelming and not overriding. Surely that is quite clear.

THE ANIMAL KINGDOM

Animal abuse

Q You have said that if the spirit is right then the material things will naturally follow and be right. How does that apply to animals in this world who are being born to be tortured, slaughtered and misused generally by man? Surely their spirit is right?

NO, that is not in the same category as the human spirit because man is given the responsibility of making the right choice; that is his free will. Man has the power of helping or hindering the evolutionary plan. Thus he has free will to decide, within limits, how he treats those who share the planet with him. Your world is full of many abuses. Not the least among them is the needless cruelty to animals and their exploitation. But it can not be otherwise if man is to progress. Were he deprived of his free will he would not have the chance to evolve his individuality and develop. So this is the crux of the whole matter.

Q It is so difficult for us to understand how this is allowed to happen.

IF you use the words "allowed to happen" it means you would rather humanity was robbed of its free will. I repeat that if humans are deprived of their free will they cease to be anything but puppets and are unable to unfold the divinity within them. Their spiritual natures will not evolve and the whole purpose of earthly life will be missed. You are put on earth because life is the nursery, the school, the training ground for the spirit. The spirit can evolve only when it is exercised by meeting challenges and overcoming them.

Q It does seem unfair to our mortal, human minds that because mankind is learning and sometimes making bad mistakes, the corollary must be the ones that pay are defenceless animals. It seems there is something amiss where man does wrong things and the animals pay.

HOW else would you have it?

Q One would think that if a man did something wrong, then retribution would be on his head rather than on an animal.

THERE is a law of compensation and retribution. You are affected spiritually and automatically by whatever good or wrong you do. None escapes the law of cause and effect. Compensation and retribution are intrinsically parts of the natural law. There is compensation for those animals on whom cruelty is wreaked, just as there is compensation for humans who suffer from the despotic acts of others for which they are not responsible.

Animal cruelty

Q We do not think that man will ever be other than cruel to animals.

NO, that is not necessarily so. There will be a gradual awareness of man's responsibility to other forms of creation. I do not say there will come a time when cruelty will finish overnight. You are evolving in an evolving world. There will be heights and depths, rises and falls, because evolution is spiral in its effect. But the overall picture is a gradual shift towards progress, otherwise there would be no evolution. You must recognise that the plan is devised by infinite wisdom and love, so that provision has been made for everything and everybody.

Q *A circle member stated that it is our fault that animals are being treated cruelly, and that gradually human beings are learning they must not eat them. To this, another visitor added: "I wish it were evident to man when he acted cruelly. He seems to get away with it."*

NOBODY gets away with it, to use your parlance. The law will always fulfil itself. If you cannot see the results in your world, I assure you they obtain in ours. You cannot in any way alter the law of cause and effect. This law is immutable, inevitable, mathematical in its operation. Effect must follow cause. Nobody gets away with it. If people could, then the Great Spirit would cease to be the perfect justice that the Great Spirit is. There is another aspect which I always stress. It is that unfortunately you can only have the short term, not the long term, view. You see only what happens in your world, but the results are outworked in ours.

Animal cruelty

THERE is much to be done to end animal cruelty. There are wars constantly being fought between the forces of good and those of greed and selfishness, between those with knowledge and those who are ignorant. And there are the shortsighted people who do not realise the part animals play in your world and that they have as much right to be there as humans have. The battles will be fought, and gradually you will win.

Animal evolution and qualities

Q *If an animal on earth develops human qualities, such as noble sentiments and intelligence, will it remain an animal without any chance of further evolution, or may it in time step into the human realm?*

EVOLUTION is part of the natural law. It has a main stream and many tributaries, but all are part of the same law. The spirit within you is in essence the same spirit within the animal. There is no difference in essence but only in degree. Potentially, being infinite, the spirit can achieve the tremendous expression latent in man or animal, but spiritually it is all part of one path. Who is to determine where spirit has branched off to be expressed through an animal, as distinct from branching off to be expressed through man? I do not see the problem there at all.

Animal evolution

IF you ask will a bird ever become a human being, the answer is no.

Q *It has been noticed there are animals who are ahead of their own natural species and exhibit more human qualities?*

THIS must be true because in all the outworking of evolution there are those who are the pioneers showing what will be achieved in the future, just as there are the laggards who have not even caught up with what should be the normal expression of evolution for their species. In human activity you get the genius, the reformer and the saint who exhibits qualities of his spiritual nature and by his gifts he can show what your world of tomorrow could be like. Similarly, there are animals who have gone some stages ahead of the others and exhibit qualities that can often compare with the finest examples of heroism and service that humans can offer.

Slow progress in animal welfare

PROGRESS is slow in some aspects and faster in others. It is man's responsibility to ensure that he is at peace with all who share the earth with him. But whatever happens, there is compensation as part of the natural law. You have the responsibility of ensuring that animals should evolve according to their path of evolution. If you abnegate your responsibilities then you must pay the price for it. Those who practice cruelty will have to pay the spiritual price for everything they do.

Animal path of evolution

Q *Does an animal evolve in a similar way to a man?*

IT follows its own path of evolution. It is part of the same pattern which is behind all evolution; it is a development. If I say to you, "Do all children evolve in the same way as their parents?" the answer is "Yes" and "No". They have a predestined pattern which they must follow, but within that there is a certain amount of free will regulated by the awareness reached at stages of unfoldment. Everything which has spirit is capable of infinite development. Animals follow their line of evolution according to the part they play in the whole process. The law of cause and effect is immutable. Whatever is must be the result of what was. All life is one. The link is the unifying spirit. The extent to which animals develop is governed by that part of the law which applies to them, as it applies to a flower, a tree, a bird, to the beasts of the field or to a human being.

Q *Higher life forms in the animal world – is there such a thing?*

NO, each animal has its own evolution to outwork. Whatever lives does so because it is spirit. Spirit is life, life is spirit. Therefore every living thing, creature, bird, fish, flower, tree, fruit, is spirit.

When you talk of higher and lower it is only a question of the stage of evolution that is reached compared with the other stages in the variegated forms of life. To the fish you may be at a higher stage of evolution, but to the hierarchy of our world you are at a lower stage.

Q *Are animals sent to earth to help mankind?*

OH yes. And mankind is sent to help them.

Animal Survival

Q *It has been said by many guides that when an animal dies it returns to a group soul. However, there is considerable evidence for animal survival. Could you enlighten us on this apparent paradox?*

THERE is individual survival for domestic animals that have had association with humans. Thus they have been helped to achieve an individual evolution that is not possible with animals who are still in a group soul, or soul group, even on earth. It is part of the wonderful relationship that can exist between humans and animals, each helping the other to develop spiritually. You help the animal that comes into your surroundings to achieve a consciousness that is more personal and individual that it otherwise would have been. It is that which survives death. But where there is not this more evolved "human" expression it joins the soul group or group soul.

Q *When the animal is no longer in contact with the person who is the cause of its progress, does it then slowly begin to return to the group soul, or alternatively is it in a kind of limbo?*

ALL the animals associated with you will be there to greet you when you come here. They will stay with you as long as it is necessary to do so, because you have helped them to gain an individuality that cannot be dissolved and this will be perpetuated. It is the individuality that persists.

Animal slaughter

Q *In order to sustain life, man has no alternative but to take plant life, fowl's eggs and cow's milk, or more savagely, slaughter animals. How can such imperative, robber sustenance be reconciled with an all-beneficent Creator without offence to that reason which you, often enough, have bidden us not to disregard?*

DON'T blame the Creator because you kill animals. The choice is yours. You do not have to kill them, but in any case the answer is very simple. Your evolution will decide for you what you should do in all these matters. If you have any doubts your conscience will give its added answer. You are responsible for what you do, and all your actions will affect your spiritual nature. An added factor is your motive. If your motive is clearly good and you have to kill, then that obviously produces an ameliorative result in your development. You cannot cheat the spiritual laws because they are based on cause and effect, reaping and sowing.

Everything you do, think and say has an automatic, inflexible result; no cheating is possible. If you do wrong consciously then you are responsible for it. Your shoulders must bear the burden that results. If you do good because you desire to do so, not for vanity's sake (because the motive then is poor), but because your soul desires to serve, then by the very fact of that happening you must be spiritually better for it. This is the law that will always operate. I have always said that it is preferable not to be involved in consuming food that bears the mark of Cain upon it. Killing is wrong, though sometimes motive must of necessity be taken into account. Those who desire spiritual mastery must be prepared to pay the price and live in harmony with the natural laws of the universe. These are spiritual in origin. The aspects of the spirit are always the same: love, compassion, tolerance, sympathy, co-operation. If you follow these principles you will find you are being led to eat aright, to drink aright, to live aright. But yours is the responsibility for deciding because the Great Spirit has endowed you with the gift of free will.

Animal reincarnation

Q *Would an animal reincarnate?*

NO, though there is a theory about the transmigration of souls.

Animal rights in spiritual context

Q *In dealing with the problems connected with animal faring Silver Birch was asked to comment on antibiotics and other drugs given to animals that are finding their way back into people who eat their flesh.*

IT is part of nature's eternal cycle that if you inflict suffering on others you must pay the price for it. You cannot be cruel to others and escape the result of your cruelty. If, because of greed, and for no other reason, you imprison the animals and deprive them to their natural rights, then you are creating a vicious circle. The law of cause and effect operates with the result that you must suffer. Only through compassion, love, mercy, kindliness and co-operation do you achieve the best that the whole of nature has to offer, whether it be animal, vegetable, flower, bird or human.

Animal abuse

Q *Why does not the spirit world interfere when it sees so many appalling atrocities committed on animals?*

BECAUSE the universe is ruled by natural laws.

Animals – responsibility towards them

ALAS, because of lack of spiritual development, there are millions of people on earth who do not realise that the spirit which animates them is the same one that animates all creatures who share the planet with them. They do not see them as spirits with earthly bodies, just as they are.

They do not realise that because they believe they are superior to the animals, they have a responsibility towards them, because the higher should always help what it believes to be the lower.

Vivisection

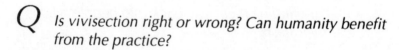 *Is vivisection right or wrong? Can humanity benefit from the practice?*

YOU have needless cruelty and terror inflicted on innocent creatures in the false belief that through this vicious means health will be attained by humans. This is not true.

I am opposed to the whole practice of experiments on animals. I see no justification for it whatsoever. Animals are placed in your guardianship and your care, and to some extent yours is the responsibility of helping their growth and their evolution. It is poor recompense for love, devotion and fidelity to inflict pain upon a helpless creature.

The healing power in many forms of nature is there waiting for you to find it. The Great Spirit has provided all that is necessary without this interference with the animal creation. Those who work from my world, who are now regarded as having some skill in the alleviation of your diseases, and even curing when others have said that recovery is impossible, do not resort to vivisection. They use herbs of the fields; they use the rays of the spirit. These do not involve any cruelty to anybody. The universe is filled with a moral purpose. Immoral purpose is contrary to the law.

Q *Are we on the verge of discovering that we cannot help people through what we call vivisection?*

I WOULD say that you can help people through vivisection, but it is not right to do so because it is contrary to everything spiritual to inflict cruelty and suffering on creatures who have done nothing to deserve it. This is where the doctors have taken the wrong path. They justify themselves by saying that man is more important than the animal. Therefore he has a right to improve his health and well-being by experimenting on these creatures. But that is wrong. What is wrong spiritually can never be condoned. You must fight to promote the welfare of all who should dwell together in amity, peace, concord and love. For love is the fulfilling of the law. You cannot have love if you wreak cruelty on others.

——o——

'Our task is to heal the sick, uplift the fallen, give strength to the weary, to guide the ones who have lost their way and banish superstition and error and flood your world with the great light of truth so that they may no longer dwell in the shadows. We pray that we may be worthy of the power that seeks to use us in all these divine tasks.' – *SILVER BIRCH*

'Always there will be offered, as you are ready, a vast richness of the spirit which cannot tarnish, fade, or ever be lost once you have acquired it. These are the prizes for you to earn, the development of your own soul, the strengthening of your own character, so that you are worthy of the light in which you dwell.' – *SILVER BIRCH*

Complete your collection

All of Silver Birch's books make superb reading, providing inspiration, illumination and perhaps occasionally consolation. Over the years, the guide answered literally thousands of questions on almost every subject imaginable. Below are further Silver Birch titles that are available. These can be read and enjoyed either individually or as a complete set, one which makes a unique collection to refer to time and time again. Each volume gives the guide's views on a comprehensive range of topics both here and hereafter.

The Silver Birch Book of Questions and Answers Compiled by Stan A. Ballard and Roger Green. This latest Silver Birch title is in easy-to-read question-and-answer form. It answers literally hundreds of points, such as "Do we reincarnate on earth?", "What are the spiritual aspects of heart transplant surgery?" and "Can euthanasia ever be right?" 240 pages. £7.99

The Seed of Truth Compiled by Tony Ortzen. Based upon two earlier out-of-print titles "Silver Birch Speaks" and "More Wisdom of Silver Birch'" which were compiled by the medium's wife, Sylvia. It contains an account of when actress Mary Pickford, "the world's sweetheart," met and questioned Silver Birch. Each chapter ends with one of the guide's uplifting prayers. 174 pages. £7.50

Lift Up Your Hearts Compiled by Tony Ortzen. This carefully chosen selection of teaching comprises the guide's wise words over a twenty-year period. Animals, a spirit view of death, mediumship and karma are just four of the many subjects explained. Features a verbatim account of when Doris Stokes and Doris Collins, two of Britain's most famous mediums, were addressed by Silver Birch. 229 pages. £7.50

Philosophy of Silver Birch Edited by Stella Storm. A former secretary to Maurice Barbanell and then chief reporter at "Psychic News," Stella   Storm covers such issues as natural law, lessons of bereavement, the responsibility of mediumship and "Healing, the greatest gift of all." Silver Birch also tells what he would say to a television audience. This popular book is now in its sixth impression. 155 pages.£7.50

More Philosophy of Silver Birch Compiled by Tony Ortzen. In easy to read question-and-answer form, of special interest are two chapters which trace man from birth to what lies Beyond. Social problems, reincarnation and science are amongst other subjects examined.   This title ends with inspiring bite-sized "Points to ponder." 253 pages.£7.50

Silver Birch Companion Edited by Tony Ortzen. Drawing upon "More Teachings of Silver Birch" and "Wisdom of Silver Birch," this volume features an account of the night Maurice Barbanell died and the days that followed. Features the repleis the guide gave to a Fleet Street editor. 159 pages. £7.50

A Voice in the Wilderness Edited by Tony Ortzen. Most of the material in this book came from handpicked cuttings at the archives of "Psychic News," though it also draws upon the out-of-print "Home Circle" and "Spirit Guidance". Read the advice the guide gave to a Member of Parliament, a senior Army chaplain and delegates at an International Spiritualist Federation cngress. 128 pages. £4.50

The Spirit Speaks Compiled by Tony Ortzen. An abridged amalgamation not only of "Silver Birch Speaks Again" and "Anthology of Silver Birch" but also important teachings that originally appeared in "Psychic News". Amongst its highlights is a word-for-word report of a meeting betwen Silver Birch and film star Merle Oberon, who was devastated when her fiance was killed in a plane crash. 142 pages. £7.50

Guidance from Silver Birch Edited by Anne Dooley. A former Fleet Street journalist, Anne Dooley later became a reporter at "Psychic News", first 'meeting' Silver Birch in 1963. Amongst subjects in this compilation are the problems of suffering and communication with the spirit world. 120 pages. £7.50

Teachings of Silver Birch Edited by A.W.Austen. First published in 1938, this classic Silver Birch title has so far run to seven impressions. It contains a fascinating Foreword by famous journalist Hannen Swaffer, after whom the Silver Birch circle was named. Silver Birch tells his own story and, as usual, answers countless questions, including life in the spirit realms. 243 pages. £7.50

Silver Birch Anthology Edited by William Naylor. Love's supreme power, what happens after we die and "Who if Silver Birch?" are just three of the topics in this absorbing book. Originally published in 1955, the philosophy within this book is still fresh, vital and valuable. 132 pages. £4.50

Light from Silver Birch Compiled by Pam Riva. Contains the last ever teachings from Silver Birch after the sudden passing of his medium Maurice Barbanell on July 17th, 1981. Also featured is Maurice Barbanell's obituary, which, ever the keen journalist, he prepared in advance. His mission with Silver Birch lasted sixty-one years. Pam Riva was the medium's secretary at "Psychic News", the paper he founded in 1932. 218 pages. £7.50

The Universe of Silver Birch By Frank Newman. This book is unique as Frank Newman has examined Silver Birch's teachings and measured them side by side with the deductions of modern science. This brings important new insights into Silver Birch's philosophy. The result is an intriguing, thought provoking volume. 118 pages. £7.50

Silver Birch Speaks Now you can hear the guide in the comfort of your own home. This sixty-minute cassette was recorded at a special sitting, during which a selection of questions was put to the guide. £4.95 (plus 60p postage and packing)

Silver Birch Meditation Print After Silver Birch was painted by psychic artist Marcel Poncin, the oil portrait had pride of place in Maurice Barbanell's London flat. Now it is available as a full colour A5-size card. The reverse contains an inspiring message from Silver Birch. £1.65 (plus 60p postage and packing)

How to order

Please send your order to Psychic Press (1995) Ltd., The Coach House, Stansted Hall, Stansted, Essex CM24 8UD. Postage and Packing is £1.00 for the first book and 50p per title thereafter. Readers outside Britain and the EU should send a list of titles required and we will let you know postage costs. Credit card orders taken by post or phone on 01279 817050. Orders can also be faxed to 01279 817051 or e-mailed to pn@snu.org.uk

Make cheques or postal orders payable to
Psychic Press (1995) Ltd.
Only sterling cheques can be accepted.